David Wilson
The Peat Inn

After Glasgow University in the 1960s David qualified as an engineer and pursued an earlier career in England - however, there was always an interest in food and a desire to return to Scotland and open his own restaurant. His "apprenticeship" formed many extra hours in other restaurants and eventually after a year of many journeys to Scotland he discovered The Peat Inn just outside Cupar, in Fife. He opened for business in November 1972. Alterations took place to extend the restaurant in 1974 and in 1987 was extended again with the addition of 8 en suite luxury bedrooms. He was the first restaurant in Scotland (not hotel) to gain a Michelin Star.

*David's contribution to Scottish cuisine has been immense and he has proved to be a great ambassador for this country. He took sourcing, preparation and presentation of food to a new level in Scotland and others followed his example. In addition, he serves the industry in an advisory capacity - I will always be grateful for his advice when I published my own **Good Food Book in 1999** as an addition to **The Good Hotel Book**.*

With the support and encouragement of his wife Patricia The Peat Inn has remained, over many years, the epitomy of gastronomic delight in Scotland. When will he retire?- hopefully not for a few years yet.

AN APPRECIATION

STEVENSONS

SCOTLAND'S
GOOD HOTEL AND FOOD BOOK
2004

Published by:
Alan Stevenson Publications
Fala
14 Cairn Slowne
Osprey Grange
Aviemore
PH22 1LG
Tel: 01479-810714
Fax: 01479-811094
Email: alan@stevensons-scotland.com
www.stevensons-scotland.com

North American Representative:
Ann Litt,
Undiscovered Britain
11978 Audubon Place
Philadelphia, PA 19116
Tel: (215) 969-0542
Fax: (215) 969-9251
Email: userann6394@cs.com
www:UndiscoveredBritain.com

ISBN 0 9526595 8 1

Price: £7.50
$12.00 from USA agent only. (Includes Canada)

Printed in Scotland: Woods of Perth Ltd.
Front Cover: The Airds Hotel, Appin, Argyll.

Alan Stevenson
Publisher

Welcome to the ninth edition of **STEVENSONS - Scotland's Good Hotel & Food Book.**

Delighted to report that Scotland has experienced another increase in visitors for 2003 driven by the domestic and European market - visitors from the USA are also on the increase once again and the outlook for 2004, depending on global events, should even be better!

*My personal choice for edition 2004 (after many miles and overnight stays) have been selected for their individuality, excellent cuisine, accommodation, character and surroundings - you will find old favourites but some hotels, for one reason or another, have been deleted. **The Good Food Book** (at rear of the book) is restricted to restaurants or restaurants with rooms who indulge in all the fine attributes of fine dining and include some of our top chefs. These attributes can also be found in many of my hotel entries. **Sharrow Bay Country House (England), Marlfield House (Ireland)** and **Ynyshir Hall (Wales)** continue as my "associate hotels". **Restaurant Michael Deane (Belfast)** continues as my "associate restaurant".*

*I am most grateful to my trade sponsors for their support, of which a list appears on page 4 (contents page). Enjoy your journey wherever you decide to go - a warm welcome is assured. Once again I look forward to my travels and the **Tenth** anniversary year of* **STEVENSONS** *in 2005.*

Photo by Yerbury of Edinburgh

STEVENSONS

SCOTLAND'S
GOOD HOTEL AND FOOD BOOK
2004

Trade Sponsors

CONTENTS

STEVENSONS

SCOTLAND'S
GOOD HOTEL AND FOOD BOOK
2004

HOW TO LOCATE A HOTEL OR RESTAURANT

1. First look at the map of **Scotland** at the beginning of the publication, **on page 8.** The place name of the hotels or restaurants I am featuring will be highlighted in bold type. Restaurants will be highlighted with a red circle. ●

2. Once you have pinpointed your location *follow along the top of the pages*, which are arranged alphabetically, until you arrive at your location.

3. If you already have the name of the hotel or restaurant and wish to know if it is included, turn to the index at the back of the book. Hotels and restaurants are listed alphabetically.

4. In some cases where hotels and restaurants are located close to major towns, they may be shown under that town with the exact location in brackets. For example, **ABERDEEN (Inverurie)**.

The Airds Hotel

5. **Hotel Price guide:** This quote is based on an overnight stay single & double. Normally this is for bed & breakfast but sometimes if dinner is included it will be indicated. (includes dinner). Also applicable to restaurants with rooms.

6. The above prices are quoted for a one night stay, but most of the establishments in this book offer reductions for stays of two or more nights. Also please enquire about seasonal bargain 'breaks'.

7. **Symbols/Awards.** Awards from VisitScotland (classification), The AA red rosettes for food and AA Red Star (Top 200 Hotels in UK) awards appear on hotel and restaurant entries. See introductory pages for a full explanation of these symbols/awards.

RECOGNITION OF LOYAL
SERVICE

SANDRA THURSTON
Breakfast Chef
Inverlochy Castle for 20 years.
Integral part of the 4 AA red
star team.

GRACE STUART
Head Housekeeper
Inver Lodge for 15 years.
Integral part of the 3 AA red
star team.

BETTY MACDONALD
Glenmoriston Arms Hotel.
35 years loyal service.

We Are... Gilchrist & Soames
We Care... About Our Customers
We Do... Everything For You
We Help... Enhance Your Guest Experience

GILCHRIST & SOAMES®

World Class Amenities For World Class Hotels

www.gilchristsoames.com
Tel: 01733 384100

STEVENSONS

SCOTLAND'S
GOOD HOTEL AND FOOD BOOK
2004

AWARDS/SYMBOLS

VisitScotland/Scottish Tourist Board

The Star System is a world-first. Quality is what determines our star awards, not a checklist of facilities. We've made your priorities our priorities.

Quality makes or breaks a visit. This is why it is only the quality of the welcome and service, the food, the hospitality, ambience and the comfort and condition of the property which earns VisitScotland Stars, not the size of the accommodation or the range of available facilities.

The quality grades awarded are:

★★★★★	Exceptional, world-class
★★★★	Excellent
★★★	Very Good
★★	Good

AA Red Rosettes 🏵 🏵 🏵 🏵 🏵

Hotels and restaurants may be awarded red rosettes to denote the quality of food they serve. It is an award scheme, not a classification scheme. They award rosettes annually on a rising scale of one to five.

AA Red Stars ★★★★★

The AA top 200 hotels in Britain and Ireland are assessed and announced annually with a red star award. They recognise the very best hotels in the country that offer consistently outstanding levels of quality, comfort, cleanliness and comfort care. Red stars are awarded on a rising scale of one to five. Restaurants with rooms also qualify for this award.

PLEASE NOTE: THESE AWARDS DO NOT NECESSARILY FORM PART OF MY OVERALL PERSONAL SELECTION OF GOOD HOTELS AND RESTAURANTS IN SCOTLAND. THEY ARE INCLUDED TO ASSIST THE VISITOR SELECT HIS/HER HOTEL OR RESTAURANT OF CHOICE. THE AWARDS ARE NOT MANDATORY FOR SELECTION TO THIS PUBLICATION.

MACDONALD THAINSTONE HOUSE

Inverurie, Aberdeenshire AB51 5NT
Tel: 01467 621643 Fax: 01467 625084
Email: thainstone@macdonald-hotels.co.uk www.macdonaldhotels.co.uk

Classical elegance blends with contemporary excellence at Thainstone House. Set in 40 acres the hotel provides everything that is luxurious offering a range of leisure activities including a Roman style indoor pool, gymnasium and jacuzzi. There is a grand portal entrance, galleried reception area and Georgian restaurant. In the Simpson restaurant table d'hôte menus are available offering a very good blend of different choices and drawing on the local resources for which the area is renowned. The 48 bedrooms, all en suite, are extremely comfortable - great care and planning reflects the high standard of hospitality here. Ideal venue for that special occasion or corporate meeting in very congenial surroundings. Although a "group hotel" there is a very informal and relaxed atmosphere throughout with a country house ambience. Thainstone makes an ideal base for touring the area and is in the heart of the whisky, castle and fishing trail. 1 AA rosette for food.

Open: *All year*	**Disabled:** *Yes*
No. Rooms: *48 En Suite 48*	**Swimming Pool/Health Club:** *Yes with beauty room*
Room telephones: *Yes*	**Conference Facilities:** *Theatre – up to 400*
TV in Rooms: *Yes*	**Price Guide:** *Single from £85.00 Double from £110.00*
Pets: *Yes*	**Location:** *Off A96 south of Inverurie.*
Children: *Yes*	

AA❀

NORWOOD HALL

Garthdee Road, Cults, Aberdeen AB15 9FX
Tel: 01224 868951 Fax: 01224 869868
Email: info@norwood-hall.co.uk www.norwood-hall.co.uk

Norwood Hall has taken on a new lease of life and has now been completely upgraded to a quality hotel. A Victorian mansion built in 1887 the hotel has great character and is situated within its own grounds just on the outside of Aberdeen at Pitfodels on the North Deeside Road. The new bedroom wing and subsequent landscaping have greatly improved this property. The new bedrooms are some of the best I have seen - opulence in every sense of the word - spacious, decorated and furnished to a very high standard. The extension fits in perfectly with the architecture of the main building. I was also very impressed with the upgrading of the public areas, dining room and library. The kitchen produces dishes which are skilfully prepared making good use of local produce – the North East is famous for its Angus beef and fresh fish from the sea. The setting is ideal for weddings and corporate business – the 5 acres of garden offer the perfect surroundings. Only 3 miles from the city centre but offers the privacy of a country house hotel. (Please mention Stevensons when making reservations).

Open: *All year.*
No. Rooms: *36 En Suite 36*
Room telephones: *Yes*
TV in Rooms: *Yes*
Pets: *Yes*   **Children:** *Yes*
Disabled: *Yes*

Swimming Pool/Health Club: *No*
Conference Facilities: *Up to 250*
Price Guide: *Single £100.00 Double from £140.00*
          (special weekend rates)
Location: *2 miles from ring road along North Deeside Road heading for Cults/Banchory. Turn left into Pitfodels Station Road to Garthdee Road.*

AA

INCHRIE CASTLE

The Trossachs, Aberfoyle, Stirlingshire FK8 3XD
Tel: 01877 382347   Fax: 01877 382785

email: enquiries@inchriecastle.co.uk   www.inchriecastle.co.uk

You will find Inchrie Castle just outside Aberfoyle in the Trossachs - one of the most popular scenic areas of Scotland. Set amongst generous garden and woodland policies the castle is steeped in Scottish history which dates back to the 17th. century. This was the domain of Rob Roy MacGregor (portrayed in the film by Liam Neeson) the famous highland chief, cattle stealer and eventually outlawed by the English. The castle has recently taken on a new "lease of life" through a major upgrading programme. There are 50 ensuite comfortable bedrooms - some with views over the valley. Many of the rooms have been refurbished completely. The food is Scottish traditional fayre with a good mix of meat and fish dishes. The hotel offers excellent facilities for conferences and weddings. Parts of the original castle remain, including quaint "neuks and crannies". There are numerous activities and places of interest to visit including Loch Lomond and Rob Roy's grave at Balquhidder. A very relaxed and friendly atmosphere prevailed throughout. Guest access to Buchanan Leisure Club.

Open: *All year*	**Swimming Pool/Health Club:** *No*
No. Rooms: *50 En Suite 50*	**Conference Facilities:** *up to 50*
Room telephones: *Yes*	**Price Guide:** *Single from £55.00 (includes dinner)*
TV in Rooms: *Yes*	*Double from £110.00 (includes dinner)*
Pets: *Arrangement* **Children:** *Yes*	**Location:** *Through main village - left over river.*
Disabled: *No*	*Castle on right.*

Scottish
TOURIST BOARD
★★★
INN

CRAIGELLACHIE HOTEL OF SPEYSIDE

Speyside, Banffshire, AB38 9SR.
Tel: 01340 881204   Fax: 01340 881253
Email: info@craigellachie.com.   www.craigellachie.com

One couldn't envisage a more idyllic setting for a hotel than that which has been enjoyed by Craigellachie since 1893. Nestling in attractive policies in the village of Craigellachie its location is right at the centre of the Whisky trail and is renowned as one of the best fishing hotels on the Spey. Known this property for many years - the major refurbishment and upgrading was completed a couple of years ago - it offers everything one would expect from a country house hotel - the award winning Quaich Bar with over 500 single malts and comfortable public areas including the library for that pre-dinner drink. 2 AA red rosettes for food are the hallmark of excellent cuisine which I have sampled myself in the intimate Ben Aigan restaurant - good use of quality local fresh produce (as one would expect in this area) and described as modern Scottish cuisine with an international flavour. Well appointed spacious bedrooms (some 4 poster) are full of charm and elegance- fine furnishings that enhance the character of each room. A relaxed informal atmosphere prevails throughout - General Manager: Duncan Elphick. Well recommended.

Open: *All year*	**Swimming Pool/Health Club:** *No*
No. Rooms: *25 En Suite 25*	**Conference Facilities:** *Up to 25 (residential only)*
Room telephones: *Yes*	**Price Guide:** *Single £100.00 (all year)*
TV in Rooms: *Yes*	*Double £120.00 - £150.00*
Pets: *Yes* **Children:** *Yes*	**Location:** *Between Grantown-On-Spey and Elgin*
Disabled: *No*	*on A95.*

AA ❀ ❀

MINMORE HOUSE HOTEL

Glenlivet, Banffshire AB37 9DB
Tel: 01807 590378   Fax: 01807 590472
email: enquiries@minmorehousehotel.com   www.minmorehousehotel.com

Minmore House is the original home of the Glenlivet whisky distilling family, and lies in the heart of the Crown Estate adjacent to the distillery of the same name. It is an elegant country house and overlooks the beautiful wide valley of the River Livet with fantastic views, and surrounded by 4 acres of sheltered landscaped gardens. The regime of Victor and Lynne Janssen (previously restaurateurs in South Africa) have made clear their intention to provide a high level of hospitality. The cuisine is a tribute to Victor who demonstrates sound technical skills with clear ambition to achieve high standards which I am sure, will soon be recognised by other agencies. Excellent use of fresh produce. The 10 en suite bedrooms and superior "Glenlivet Suite" (most with stunning views) are spacious with every comfort - public rooms offer relaxation with roaring log fires in winter. This is more a house than a hotel and Lynne's expert front of house skills ensure you have a memorable stay. Visits to distilleries and "castle trail" are popular. In addition there is an outdoor, unheated swimming pool. Sample the vast range of malt whiskies available in the oak panelled bar and enjoy a very relaxed and friendly atmosphere. Highly recommended.

Open: *Mid March - October & December*	**Swimming Pool/Health Club:** *Outdoor/unheated s/pool*
No. Rooms: *10 En Suite 10*	**Conference Facilities:** *No*
Room telephones: *Yes*	**Price Guide:** *Single £60.00*
TV in Rooms: *No*	*Double £120.00-£140.00 Suite £160.00*
Pets: *Arrangement* **Children:** *Over 8*	**Location:** *A95 from Grantown-On-Spey for 15 mls.*
Disabled: *No*	*Take B9008 & follow signs*

SUMMER ISLES HOTEL

Achiltibuie, Ross-shire IV26 2YG
Tel: 01854 622282   Fax: 01854 622251
Email: summerisleshotel@aol.com   www.summerisleshotel.com

The road leading to The Summer Isles Hotel at Achiltibuie is 10 miles north of Ullapool. You approach Achiltibuie under the watchful eye of Stac Poly and quite magnificent scenery. The hotel itself commands a delightful spot in the village with spectacular views to The Summer Isles. The Irvine family have run this individual but sophisticated hotel since the late 60's and hosts Mark and Geraldine have established an oasis of civilisation hidden away in stunningly beautiful, but still wild and untouched landscape. This is certainly the place to indulge yourself and Chef Chris Firth-Bernard produces mouth-watering dishes using only locally produced ingredients or fish netted nearby. In addition to the "boat house" suite (bedroom reached by spiral staircase) 2 new sea-view suites have been created which are very spacious and offer every possible comfort. Eating well, sleeping well and moving about in beautiful surroundings is a therapy for which many return year after year. Scottish Chef of Year Award 1998. Well worth the visit and highly recommended.

Open: *April 1st-October 14th*	**Disabled:** *Unsuitable*
No. Rooms: *13 En Suite 12*	**Swimming Pool/Health Club:** *No*
Room telephones: *Yes*	**Conference Facilities:** *No*
TV in Rooms: *No*	**Price Guide:** *Single from £70.00 Double from £115.00-£170.00*
Pets: *By arrangement*	**Location:** *A835 to Ullapool. 10 miles north of Ullapool turn*
Children: *Over 8*	*left onto single track road to Achiltibuie. 15 miles to village.*

THE AIRDS HOTEL
Port Appin, Appin, Argyll PA38 4DF
Tel: 01631 730236 Fax: 01631 730535
Email: airds@airds-hotel.com www.airds-hotel.com

A stunning property overlooking Lismore island the name is well known in hotel circles as one of the premier properties in Scotland. Sold in December 2002, and after several visits, it is quite evident that resident proprietors Shaun and Jenny McKivragan (delightful hosts) will uphold the very high standards for which this hotel has been known in the past. At one time an old ferry inn it has become a mecca for travellers from all over the world who indulge themselves in the finest traditions of hotel keeping. There is a "feel good" factor when you enter this hotel with fresh flowers and extremely friendly and efficient staff. All 12 bedrooms are different - tastefully furnished to a high standard. Public areas (1 smoking) have a "homely" feel about them with fine artwork on walls and comforting fires conveying an atmosphere of feeling at ease with the world. Diners expectations (Head Chef J. Paul Burns) are fully met with a range of dishes executed with high technical skills producing a depth of flavour (good innovation) and use of seasonal produce. Excellent wine list. Sometimes forgotten I was very impressed with the housekeeping - fresh, bright and absolutely spotless. Its a tribute to Shaun and Jenny who had a hard act to follow but they will succeed. VisitScotland 4 stars small hotel graded with 3 AA red rosettes for food and AA Top 200 with 3 red stars.

Open: *All year except 3 weeks in Jan*	**Swimming Pool/Health Club:** *No*
No. Rooms: *12 En Suite 12*	**Conference Facilities:** *No*
Room telephones: *Yes*	**Price Guide:** *Double £230.00-£360.00 Full suite*
TV in Rooms: *Yes*	*Single £160.00-£255.00 (All include dinner)*
Pets: *By arrangement* **Children:** *Yes*	**Location:** *16 mls north of Oban on A828. 25 mls*
Disabled: *2 rms (limited)*	*south of Fort William.*

LOCH MELFORT HOTEL & RESTAURANT

Arduaine, by Oban, Argyll PA34 4XG
Tel: 01852 200233   Fax: 01852 200214
email: reception@lochmelfort.co.uk   www.lochmelfort.co.uk

This is a spectacular location on the west coast of Scotland with views over Asknish Bay to Jura. Resident proprietors Nigel and Kyle Schofield have implemented a major refurbishment programme which will take this hotel to a new level. Bedrooms are being upgraded, the dining area (with magnificent views) is being completely revamped and public areas of the hotel are a delight with soft furnishings and a warmth which exudes peace and contentment. The award of 2 AA red rosettes for food indicates the high standards of cuisine achieved - technical skills in the kitchen which displays judgement in combining and balancing ingredients with good use of seasonal fresh produce. An excellent, award-winning wine list complements the fine dining experience. Light meals and afternoon teas are available in the Bistro. The famous Arduaine Gardens are situated next to the hotel - owned by the National Trust for Scotland these gardens are known to enthusiasts all over the world. Although the area is known for its outdoor activities (yachting is popular) it is the ideal base to explore the area. South to Campbeltown or north to Fort William. An excellent choice for an extended stay.

Open: *All year*	**Swimming Pool/Health Club:** *No*
No. Rooms: *26 En Suite 26*	**Conference Facilities:** *up to 40*
Room telephones: *Yes*	**Price Guide:** *Single from £55.00-£79.00*
TV in Rooms: *Yes*	*Double from £70.00-£158.00 (2 superior*
Pets: *Yes* **Children:** *Yes*	*rooms)*
Disabled: *No*	**Location:** *A816 - 19 miles south of Oban*

Scottish TOURIST BOARD ★★★★ HOTEL   **AA** ✿ ✿

CULZEAN CASTLE
The Eisenhower Apartment
Maybole, Ayrshire, KA19 8LE
Tel: 01655 884455 Fax: 01655 884503
email: culzean@nts.org.uk www. culzeancastle.net

Culzean Castle, a National Trust for Scotland property, is located on the west coast of Scotland just south of Ayr. Its position, perched on a clifftop with magnificent views over to the Isle of Arran is spectacular. The property is steeped in Scottish history and was gifted to the National Trust for Scotland by the Kennedy Family in 1945. Charles Kennedy, the 5th. Marquess of Ailsa, also gifted the top floor of the castle to President Eisenhower as a token of thanks after WW2 - known as The Eisenhower Apartment. Bedrooms offer every comfort for the discerning traveller - very spacious with fine antique furnishings and breathtaking views. A rare collection of Kennedy family portraits can be viewed in the State Dining Room on the ground floor of the castle whilst hunting prints keep you company in the fine dining room and, although this is a reminder of a bygone era, the cuisine has kept pace with modern trends - menus offer the best of fresh seasonal produce with traditional Scottish dishes - the home baking served with afternoon teas in the round drawing room a real feature. This is the ideal location for family gatherings or company meetings - complete privacy in a perfect setting. Leisure activities include golf at nearby Turnberry and Troon. No smoking establishment. The ideal retreat - your hosts Jonathan and Susan Cardale.

Open: *All year except Christmas & Feb.*	**Swimming Pool/Health Club:** *No*
No. Rooms: *6 En Suite 5*	**Conference Facilities:** *Up to 90*
Room telephones: *Yes*	**Price Guide:** *Single £150.00 – £250.00*
TV in Rooms: *No (Drawing Room)*	*Double £225.00 – £375.00*
Pets: *No* **Children:** *By enquiry*	**Location:** *From Glasgow A77 towards Ayr.*
Disabled: *Limited*	*Castle is 12 miles south of Ayr on A719.*

Susan Russell
Head Gardener
Culzean Country Park

Susan is originally from Glasgow and her pre entry into the Scottish Agricultural College in Ayr was spent at the Botanical Gardens in Glasgow. She gained an Ordinary National Diploma in amenity horticulture, spending her placement year at Hyde Hall in Essex. Before taking up the post of First Gardener at Culzean Country Park in 1984 she worked at Castle Kennedy Gardens, Stranraer, latterly as Head Gardener. She became Head Gardener at Culzean in 1989. Her main interests are herbaceous plants, half hardy perennials and viticulture.

BALGONIE COUNTRY HOUSE

Braemar Place, Ballater, Royal Deeside AB35 5NQ
Tel/Fax: 013397 55482
Email: balgoniech@aol.com www.royaldeesidehotels.com

Secluded Edwardian country house on the outskirts of Ballater, Balgonie House is situated in 4 acres of mature gardens and woodland. A very homely atmosphere here with 9 delightful, fresh and comfortable bedrooms, individually decorated and furnished to a high standard. The cuisine was the highlight of my stay here - expectation was high and fully met. Game terrine followed by loin of lamb (pink & lean) and to finish ice cream with candied peel, pistachios and glace cherries. This is what charismatic host John Finnie calls the heart of the hotel, and rightly so. Excellent wine list to complement such fine food. Sitting-room and bar (with good range of malts to savour) are furnished in keeping with the style of the building. Not far from Balmoral Castle, in the heart of the Dee valley, this is a haven for fishermen, golfers and walkers. The outstanding garden policies are a tribute to some hard work from resident hosts, John and Priscilla Finnie. A very pleasant and peaceful stay. AA top 200 hotel with 2 red stars and 2 rosettes awarded for food. Within short walking distance of the village and 40 miles from Aberdeen.

Open: *February - December*	**Swimming Pool/Health Club:** *No*
No. Rooms: *9 En Suite 9*	**Conference Facilities:** *Small groups*
Room telephones: *Yes*	**Price Guide:** *Single £110.00 (includes dinner)*
TV in Rooms: *Yes*	*Double £190.00 (includes dinner)*
Pets: *On request* **Children:** *Yes*	**Location:** *40 mls from Aberdeen on A93. Hotel on*
Disabled: *No*	*outskirts of village on west side.*

AA✿✿
★★

HILTON CRAIGENDARROCH

Braemar Road, Ballater, Royal Deeside AB35 5XA
Tel: 013397 55858 Fax: 013397 55447

reservations_craigendarroch@hilton.com www.hilton.co.uk

Although I stayed at Craigendarroch when it opened in 1985 it was nice to return for another stay in 2003. There have been changes as one would expect but Hilton have managed to retain all the qualities of a country house hotel catering for the needs not only of the visitor, but the corporate and family requirements. Formerly the magnificent highland residence of the Keiller Family (of marmalade fame) this property is an elegant building retaining all the charm and character of a country retreat. The view is dominated by the river Dee cutting a majestic swathe through the valley below. To the west is Balmoral and the towering peak of Lochnagar. The hotel with its oak panelled hallway and library has everything one could want - cuisine of the highest order served in the Oaks Restaurant or more informally in The Club House. Accommodation can only be described as luxurious - some of the rooms with their own suites and patios - whilst self-catering holiday lodges are also available. The leisure facilities have always proved popular here - 2 swimming pools, one with spa bath plus a host of other activities. The Dee Valley is one of the most scenic parts of Scotland. Your host Michael Pickford.

Open: *All year*	**Swimming Pool/Health Club:** *Yes*
No. Rooms: *45 En Suite 45*	**Conference Facilities:** *Up to 120*
Room telephones: *Yes*	**Price Guide:** *Single (B&B)* **£66.00-£97.00** *per person*
TV in Rooms: *Yes*	*Double (B&B)* **£46.00-£77.00** *per person*
Pets: *No* **Children:** *Yes*	**Location:** *On A93 western end of Ballater. (Balmoral end of*
Disabled: *Yes*	*the village).*

BANCHORY LODGE HOTEL

Banchory, Kincardineshire AB31 3HS
Tel: 01330 822625 Fax: 01330 825019
Email: enquiries@banchorylodge.co.uk www.banchorylodge.co.uk

This Deeside hotel which was formerly an 18th century coaching inn is spectacularly situated on the banks of the River Dee. The gardens reflect the care and attention taken by resident proprietor Margaret Jaffray with sweeping lawns down to the river bank and an abundance of flowers (especially the daffodils in spring). This care and attention continues its theme within the hotel where all the best qualities can be savoured. The bedrooms are very spacious and comfortable - designed with considerable flair and imagination. Many have views over the river. The dining room is a masterpiece. Creative menus include Dee salmon and Aberdeen Angus beef as one would expect in this area. "Block bookings" for weddings (ideal venue) and corporate meetings are welcomed - in this way it does not interfere with other guests who find this hotel a haven of tranquillity. An old favourite of mine, I have some wonderful memories of this establishment in years past. A tribute to Margaret and her staff in upholding very fine traditions of hotel keeping. Fishing and shooting arrangements can be made through the hotel. RAC Blue Ribbon.

Open: *All year*
No. Rooms: *22 En Suite 22*
Room telephones: *Yes*
TV in Rooms: *Yes*
Pets: *Yes* **Children:** *Yes*
Disabled: *No*

Swimming Pool/Health Club: *No*
Conference Facilities: *Up to 30*
Price Guide: *Single £75.00 Double £130.00*
Location: *A93 North Deeside road from Aberdeen. Turn down Dee Street from Main Street - 400 yards - hotel on your left.*

AA❀

SKIRLING HOUSE

Skirling, Biggar, Lanarkshire ML12 6HD
Tel: 01899 860274   Fax: 01899 860255

email: enquiry@skirlinghouse.com   www.skirlinghouse.com

This house, built in 1908, was designed by the famous architect Ramsay Traquair for Lord Carmichael as a country retreat. Skirling is a small attractive village just outside Biggar on the A72 to Peebles and the property is situated by the village green. The house has retained the original theme with carvings, rich fabrics, antiques and fine paintings - a feature is the 16th century Florentine carved ceiling which is much admired by guests. Bob and Isobel Hunter have made this an oasis of great comfort, quality cuisine and hospitality and there is a very informal but friendly and relaxing atmosphere. The award of 5 stars Guest House from VisitScotland is fully merited - bedrooms are tastefully decorated in keeping with the house and offer every comfort. The house menus (dinner is a set menu) change daily and make excellent use of fresh seasonal produce from the garden. Good selection and a sound quality of food with fine farmhouse cheeses. Meals are served in the conservatory with views over the magnificent lawn and gardens to the rear. (also with herb garden) A very skilled operation here and highly recommended. Only a short distance from Edinburgh. No smoking throughout.

Open: *March - December*	**Price Guide:** *Single £72.50-£75.00 (inc. dinner)*
No. Rooms: *5 En Suite 5*	*B&B £47.50-£50.00*
Room telephones: *Yes*	*Double £125.00-£130.00 (inc. dinner*
TV in Rooms: *Yes*	*B&B £75.00-£80.00*
Pets: *Yes* **Children:** *Yes*	**Location:** *2 mls from Biggar on A72 overlooking*
Disabled: *Yes*	*village green.*

THE ROYAL HOTEL

Bridge of Allan, Stirlingshire FK9 4HG
Tel: 01786 832284 Fax: 01786 834377
Email: stay@royal-stirling.co.uk www.royal-stirling.co.uk

Situated on the main thoroughfare The Royal Hotel is an impressive Victorian mansion built in 1842 close to historic Stirling and with easy access from the M9 motorway. Recently there was a massive refurbishment programme undertaken to improve all facilities with the comfort of the guest a main priority. Bedrooms have been carefully restored to a high quality of comfort as have public rooms and functional areas. The kitchen deserves special merit for its use of local produce combined with an imaginative flair to produce dishes of good quality Scottish cuisine. One can dine informally and prices are reasonable and complemented with a fine cellar of wines to your taste. Well experienced in the conference market, The Royal is well placed and can accommodate up to 100 delegates with car parking for 80 vehicles. I found the staff very receptive and friendly and took time to resolve any questions that I had - there are many leisure activities for the sporting enthusiast including golf at Gleneagles, St. Andrews or Carnoustie. Steeped in Scotland's Heritage there are many sites to visit and The Royal is an ideal touring base.

Open: *All year*	**Swimming Pool/Health Club:** *No*
No. Rooms: *32 En Suite 32*	**Conference Facilities:** *Full facilities, up to 100 delegates.*
Room telephones: *Yes*	**Price Guide:** *Single from £65.00 Double from £90.00*
TV in Rooms: *Yes*	*(terms & short breaks available)*
Pets: *No* **Children:** *Yes*	**Location:** *Centre of town - just off M9 between Dunblane*
Disabled: *Limited*	*and Stirling.*

AA❀

DUISDALE COUNTRY HOUSE HOTEL

Sleat, Isle of Skye, Inverness-shire IV43 8QW

Tel: 01471 833202   Fax: 01471 833404

Email: marie@duisdalehotel.demon.co.uk   www.duisdale.com

Originally built as a hunting lodge in 1857 Duisdale is situated in the south part of the island known as the 'garden of Skye'. It commands a stunning position overlooking Sleat to Knoydart within 25 acres of magnificent gardens complete with putting and croquet lawn. Resident proprietor Marie Campbell, who arrived here 7 years ago, has performed a miracle with this property. The refurbishment has been a great success with 17 very comfortable en suite bedrooms and a dining experience not to be missed. Marie, who trained in Paris at the Ritz-Escoffier and well known in culinary circles produces superb dishes making excellent use of the local produce on hand. Menus are creative and well balanced. The perfect ambience of the dining room added to the enjoyment which, in fact, prevails throughout the whole hotel - public rooms are finely furnished and spacious with roaring log fire to retain the charm and warmth of this establishment. Duisdale can be reached via the ferry from Mallaig and Glenelg (the route I prefer) or by road over the Skye bridge via Broadford. An ideal base to tour around the island of Skye. Marie has been awarded 2 AA red rosettes for food.

Open: *Easter-October*	**Swimming Pool/Health Club:** *No*
No. Rooms: *17 En Suite 17*	**Conference Facilities:** *Up to 30*
Room telephones: *Yes*	**Price Guide:** *Single £65.00 Double £80.00-£150.00*
TV in Rooms: *No*	**Location:** *By ferry from Mallaig and Glenelg.*
Pets: *No* **Children:** *Yes*	*By road over the Skye Bridge via Broadford to Sleat*
Disabled: *Dinner only*	*(South Skye)*

AA 🌸 🌸

ROMAN CAMP COUNTRY HOUSE

Off Main Street, Callander, Perthshire FK17 8BG
Tel: 01877 330003 Fax: 01877 331533
Email: mail@roman-camp-hotel.co.uk www.romancamp-hotel.co.uk

This is an outstanding property - originally built as a hunting lodge in 1625 for the Dukes of Perth. It is set in 20 acres of beautiful parkland and is well hidden from the main part of the town of Callander offering privacy and isolation. Its geographic position, however, is ideal for touring the Trossachs, which is an area of outstanding beauty in Scotland. Each of the 14 hotel bedrooms has its own distinctive theme with period furniture and all are equipped with the facilities of a VisitScotland 4 Star Hotel - now AA 3 Red Stars and Top 200. 3 AA red rosettes are the hallmark of the cuisine - based on an ever changing menu and the use of fresh local ingredients. The public rooms are a joy with 16th century oak panelling in the library. On my many visits there is always the glow of a warm log fire no matter the weather which adds to your well being. The spacious dining room, with fine linen and cutlery, is a delight and when required can accomodate a conference or wedding party for up to 100. Resident proprietors Eric and Marion Brown are renowned for their attention to detail and a warm welcome to all.

Open: *All year*	**Swimming Pool/Health Club:** *No*
No. Rooms: *14 En Suite 14*	**Conference Facilities:** *Up to 100*
Room telephones: *Yes*	**Price Guide:** *Single from £90-£140. Double from £110-£200.*
TV in Rooms: *Yes*	**Location:** *East End of Callander. Main Street from Stirling*
Pets: *Yes* **Children:** *Yes*	*turn left down drive for 300 yards.*
Disabled: *Yes*	

AA ❀ ❀ ❀
★ ★ ★

PITTODRIE HOUSE

Chapel of Garioch, Near Pitcaple, Aberdeenshire AB51 5HS
Tel: 01467 681444   Fax: 01467 681648
Email: pittodrie@macdonald-hotels.co.uk   www.macdonaldhotels.co.uk

Pittodrie House is an imposing turreted Scottish baronial style mansion dating back to 1480. It stands at the foot of Bennachie within a 2000 acre estate and the grounds around the building are something to behold. As one might expect the hotel is a popular venue for weddings. The ancestral home of Theo Smith the family paintings and antiques have been retained in all the reception rooms and some of the bedrooms to keep the atmosphere of a country house rather than a hotel. You can make yourself at home in front of log fires and taste one of more than 90 malt whiskies stocked in the comfortable bar. All 27 bedrooms are furnished to a high standard, all are en suite and have all the amenities you would expect from a modern hotel. The orangery is an extension of the dining room where the menu is changed daily. Specialities are game, smoked and fresh fish and Aberdeen Angus beef. Vegetables and herbs are grown in the walled garden. Plans are underway for a major development programme which will include a golf course, leisure facilities and a refurbishment of the hotel and other buildings. Watch this space...

Open: *All year*	**Swimming Pool/Health Club:** *No*
No. Rooms: *27 En Suite 27*	**Conference Facilities:** *Yes*
Room telephones: *Yes*	**Price Guide:** *Single from £80.00 Double from £105.00*
TV in Rooms: *Yes*	**Location:** *Off A96 just north of Pitcaple. 20 miles north of*
Pets: *Yes* **Children:** *Yes*	*Aberdeen.*
Disabled: *Unsuitable*	

LOCH NESS LODGE HOTEL

Drumnadrochit, Inverness-shire IV63 6TU
Tel: 01456 450342   Fax: 01456 450429
Email: info@lochness-hotel.com   www.lochness-hotel.com

Dating back to around 1740, this unusual hotel is synonymous with the famous Loch from which it takes its name. Once the home of a colonial tea planter, it stands in eight acres of delightful woodland grounds. Situated 14 miles from Inverness, it is a favourite spot for tourists. The hotel offers elegant en suite bedrooms and fresh imaginatively prepared food. The restaurant serves prime Aberdeen Angus beef, West Coast seafood from Mallaig and Kinlochbervie, local venison, wild mushrooms and fresh garden vegetables. The hotel is linked to the Visitor Centre with its unique exhibition which attracts people from around the world. The management are now actively marketing their corporate facilities - this is the ideal venue for such an occasion away from the "hustle and bustle" of city life and a short drive from Inverness. Two open log fires, friendly staff, outstanding cuisine and first class service make a holiday at the Loch Ness Lodge Hotel a memorable experience. Urquhart Castle close by offers one of the best views of Loch Ness. Your host : Gillian Skinner.

Open: *April-Oct.*	**Swimming Pool/Health Club:** *No*
No. Rooms: *27 En Suite 27*	**Conference Facilities:** *Max. 120.*
Room telephones: *Yes*	**Price Guide:** *Single £40.00-£60.00*
TV in Rooms: *Yes*	*Double £80.00-£120.00*
Pets: *No* **Children:** *Yes*	**Location:** *14 miles south of Inverness on Fort William Road.*
Disabled: *Yes*	

THE BUCHANAN ARMS HOTEL & LEISURE CLUB

Drymen, by Loch Lomond, Stirlingshire G63 0BQ
Tel: 01360 660588   Fax: 01360 660943
emal: enquiries@buchananarms.co.uk   www.buchananarms.co.uk

In the heart of a conservation village near Loch Lomond, the Buchanan seems to soak up the mood of the beautiful surrounding countryside. A very attractive former coaching inn standing prominent in the picturesque village, it is situated between the vibrant City of Glasgow and historic Stirling, making it the perfect base for touring. Recently acquired by Stonefield Castle Group, the new owners are to be complemented on their programme of refurbishment and upgrading which was evident on my visit. The bedrooms, all en-suite, are fresh, bright and spacious. Superior rooms have traditional furnishings, some with four poster beds. Tapestries Restaurant within the Hotel has long had a reputation for good food and convivial surroundings. Service was swift and efficient with some innovative dishes to tempt the palate. The modern leisure facilities are a feature - swimming pool, sauna, jacuzzi, squash courts and 'state-of-the-art' gymnasium and exercise area. The function suite is popular for business meetings, seminars and weddings. This is a 'well rounded' hotel catering for all modern day requirements whether family, business, tourist or simply a very pleasant day out to enjoy afternoon tea. A careful blend of character and comfort. Your host : David Kenyon.

Open: *All year*	**Swimming Pool/Health Club:** *Yes*
No. Rooms: *52 En Suite 52*	**Conference Facilities:** *Up to 150*
Room telephones: *Yes*	**Price Guide:** *Single from £60.00*
TV in Rooms: *Yes*	*Double from £110.00*
Pets: *Arrangement* **Children:** *Yes*	**Location:** *Main Street/Drymen by Loch Lomond*
Disabled: *No*	

HILTON DUNKELD HOUSE

Dunkeld, Perthshire PH8 0HX
Tel: 01350 727771   Fax: 01350 728924
Email: reservations_dunkeld@hilton.com   www.hiltondunkeldhouse.co.uk

Although a "group/chain hotel" this is a very fine country house built by the 7th. Duke of Atholl in the last century. Just 12 miles north of Perth it stands on the banks of the Tay, one of Scotland's finest salmon rivers and is surrounded by 280 acres of magnificent Perthshire countryside. Normally associated with city hotels Hilton have managed to maintain the perfect country house ambience here and have implemented a carefully restructured investment programme - bedrooms (all en suite) with some overlooking the Tay itself, are extremely comfortable - there is a good "mix" of double/twin & family rooms. "Extra"touches add to the attraction of each room. Head chef should be complemented on a wide range of dishes -mainly modern Scottish cuisine, skilfully prepared and adept at some innovation. The leisure and sporting facilities here are unrivalled amongst most country house hotels - salmon fishing, clay pigeon shoot, 4 x 4 off road driving, Livingwell Health Club and indoor pool to mention a few. There is emphasis here on staff training (lacking in some other establishments I am afraid) and it is quite evident - testimony indeed to Hilton and the work of General Manager Philip Rolfe over a 4 year period. Long may it continue.

Open: *All year*	**Swimming Pool/Health Club:** *Yes*
No. Rooms: *96 En Suite 96*	**Conference Facilities:** *Up to 90 delegates*
Room telephones: *Yes*	**Price Guide:** *Double £116.00-£130.00.*
TV in Rooms: *Yes*	**Location:** *A9 12 miles north of Perth – through village of*
Pets: *Yes (in kennels)* **Children:** *Yes*	*Dunkeld and turn left, through gateway.*
Disabled: *Yes*	

THE HOUSE OF
BRUAR
Established 1993

THE HOME OF COUNTRY CLOTHING

**Having recently been awarded 5 star tourist board status,
The House of Bruar is Scotland's most prestigious country store.**

in it's unique environment The House of Bruar includes mens and ladies Country Clothing Halls, a ladies
accessory department and Scotland's largest cashmere and knitwear hall. The most unusual and individual
e found in the Country Gift shop and the library stocks many different book titles. The comprehensive foo
ch includes a delicatessen, promotes the best of Scottish/British produce alongside delicacies from around
rld. After an afternoon stroll up the famous Bruar Falls walk, why not round off a day at The House of Bru
with a delicious meal in the excellent Rod and Reel restaurant.

Opening in the spring of 2004 will be a Fine Arts Centre incorporating
period furniture and pictures and including contemporary wildlife exhibits.

ve a day out in Highland Perthshire and visit The House of Bruar, Blair Castle and Pitlochry Festival Thea

**For a copy of our latest mail order catalogue, which brings a carefully selected range of products
direct to your home, please phone, fax, write or e-mail.**
he House of Bruar By Blair Atholl Perthshire PH18 5TW Tel 01796 483236 Fax 01796 48339
E-mail office@houseofbruar.com www.houseofbruar.com

KINNAIRD

Kinnaird Estate, By Dunkeld, Perthshire PH8 0LB
Tel: 01796 482440   Fax: 01796 482289
Email: enquiry@kinnairdestate.com   www.kinnairdestate.com

A member of the prestigious Relais & Chateaux Kinnaird is set on a bluff in the middle of its own 9000 acres overlooking the Tay River Valley. The building has been restored to its former glory by its owner Mrs Constance Ward. The gardens are immaculate and there is a feeling of well being when you drive up to the front of the house. Superb cuisine can be enjoyed in two exquisite dining rooms, one of which overlooks the River Tay. As one would expect the bedrooms have been individually decorated with fabrics and furnishings to complement the size of the rooms and the views. The large private bathrooms have been retained in the traditional style of the house. Public rooms are furnished almost entirely with fine and rare pieces of furniture, china and pictures. Kinnaird also offers a wide range of outdoor pursuits. Although a hotel Kinnaird has been described as a comfortable, beautiful but cosy home that happens to be a hotel. It upholds the finest traditions of hotel keeping. AA Top 200 RAC Gold Ribbon. (Please mention Stevensons when making reservations).

Open: *All year*	**Swimming Pool/Health Club:** *No*
No. Rooms: *9 En Suite 9*	**Conference Facilities:** *Small business meeting Director level*
Room telephones: *Yes*	**Price Guide:** *Double May-Oct.* **£425.00** *all rooms*
TV in Rooms: *Yes*	*Nov.-Apr.* **£325.00.** *All rates inc dinner.*
Pets: *In kennels* **Children:** *Over 12*	**Location:** *2 miles north of Dunkeld on A9 – take B898*
Disabled: *Yes*	*turn off.*

AA ❀ ❀ ❀
★★★

RAMNEE HOTEL
Victoria Road, Forres, Moray IV36 3BN
Tel: 01309 672410 Fax: 01309 673392
Email: ramneehotel@btconnect.com www.ramneehotel.net

This fine Edwardian mansion built in 1907 is situated in landscaped gardens to the east of the Royal Burgh of Forres. The Ramnee enjoys a certain amount of isolation but is in easy reach of the town centre which is famous for its parkland floral displays and architectural qualities. I knew this hotel before the arrival of resident director Garry Dinnes but he has brought an expertise with him that has transformed this hotel to a high quality establishment. This is reflected with a VisitScotland 4 star classification. The bedrooms are a delight, (with 4 poster if required) - elegant, and very comfortable, all with en suite facilities - many have views over the Moray Firth. Scottish cuisine with a slight French influence using only the best of local produce - menus are varied to suit your appetite - there is imagination and flair used in the preparation and you will not be disappointed whether dining formally or taking a bar lunch/supper. Golfing is high on the list of sporting activities in this area and businessmen make good use of the conference/seminar facilities. There is a friendly atmosphere which radiates throughout the hotel.

Open: *All year.*
No. Rooms: *20 En Suite 20*
Room telephones: *Yes*
TV in Rooms: *Yes*
Pets: *Yes* **Children:** *Yes*
Disabled: *Unsuitable.*

Swimming Pool/Health Club: *No*
Conference Facilities: *Theatre up to 100.*
Price Guide: *Single £60-£80; Double £75-£120.*
Location: *A96 Inverness-Aberdeen off by-pass at roundabout to east side of Forres - 500 yards on right.*

ALLT-NAN-ROS HOTEL

Onich, by Fort William, Inverness-shire PH33 6RY

Tel: 01855 821210 Fax: 01855 821462

email: reception@allt-nan-ros.co.uk www.allt-nan-ros.co.uk

Allt-nan-Ros is Gaelic for "the burn of the roses" and the name derives from the enchanting cascading stream which passes through the gardens of the hotel and on into Loch Leven & Loch Linnhe. From an elevated site the hotel enjoys quite exceptional views across spectacular mountain scenery, and along the loch, beyond Appin and towards the Isle of Mull. This Victorian house, owned by the MacLeod family has been tastefully upgraded into its present form - en suite bedrooms with quality furnishings - some superior rooms with views over the loch. The lounge, foyer and dining room are richly furnished in traditional style, where fresh flowers abound. The cuisine is French with a strong west highland flavour. Accolades include a 4 star rating from VisitScotland and 2 AA red rosettes for food. Fort William is only 10 miles north of Onich and 5 miles from historic Glencoe and there is easy access to the Ardnamurchan Peninsula via the Corran ferry. Ongoing refurbishment and it just gets better and better! - entry to the Good Hotel Guide (UK) this year.

Open: *Closed Mid./Nov.-29th Dec.*
No. Rooms: *20 En Suite 20*
Room telephones: *Yes*
TV in Rooms: *Yes*
Pets: *Yes* **Children:** *Yes*
Disabled: *Unsuitable*

Swimming Pool/Health Club: *No*
Conference Facilities: *No*
Price Guide: *£70.00-£85.00 Dinner Bed and Breakfast.*
Location: *On A82, 10 miles south of Fort William.*

AA

MIS EN BOUTEILLE AU CHÂTEAU

CHÂTEAU MARGAUX
GRAND VIN

1983
PREMIER GRAND CRU CLASSÉ

MARGAUX

APPELLATION MARGAUX CONTRÔLÉE
SCA CHATEAU MARGAUX PROPRIÉTAIRE A MARGAUX · FRANCE

HILDON

AN ENGLISH
NATURAL MINERAL WATER
OF EXCEPTIONAL TASTE

DELIGHTFULLY STILL

Hildon Ltd., Broughton, Hampshire SO20 8DQ. ☎ 01794 301

The King and I

INVERLOCHY CASTLE
Torlundy, Fort William PH33 6SN
Tel: 01397 702177 Fax: 01397 702953 USA Toll Free Tel: 1-888 424 0106
Email: info@inverlochy.co.uk www.inverlochycastlehotel.com

This is truly an outstanding property set in magnificent landscaped gardens just North of Fort William. It nestles below Ben Nevis in stunning Highland scenery. Fine decorations throughout befit the Victorian proportions of the rooms and reflect the atmosphere of a former era. Awarded the RAC Gold Ribbon and 3 AA red rosettes the cuisine is quite exceptional with food prepared with considerable flair, imagination and originality. As a member of the prestigious Relais & Châteaux this establishment retains all the finest traditions of hotel keeping. A stroll through the walled garden or a spot of fishing in the nearby loch offer relaxation - for the more outgoing there are numerous walks in the area and the ski-ing facilities are some of the best in Scotland. During her visit in 1873 Queen Victoria wrote in her diaries "I never saw a lovelier or more romantic spot". Inverlochy offers its guests a warm welcome, peace and seclusion, with cuisine and wine cellar of the highest standard. AA Top 200. (Please mention Stevensons when making reservations). General Manager : Niall Edmondson.

Open: *Late Feb-early Jan*	**Swimming Pool/Health Club:** *No*
No. Rooms: *17 (2 suites) All En Suite*	**Conference Facilities:** *Director level.*
Room telephones: *Yes*	**Price Guide:** *Single £205-£290; Double/Twin £330-£435;*
TV in Rooms: *Yes*	*Suite £440-£550.*
Pets: *By arrangement* **Children:** *Yes*	**Location:** *3 miles north of Fort William. In the village of*
Disabled: *No.*	*Torlundy on A82.*

THE FACTORS INN & HEATHER COTTAGE

Inverlochy Estate, Torlundy, Fort William, Inverness-shire PH33 6SN

Tel: 01397 701420 Fax: 01397 701421

Email: infor@inverlochy.co.uk www.inverlochycastlehotel.com

The Factors Inn is situated at the north entrance to Inverlochy Castle just off the main A82 at Torlundy. Formerly The Factors House the property has been transformed to an "inn" with 4 non-smoking, quality en suite bedrooms - the interior has received a major refurbishment and operates independently of the castle. In addition the grounds have been extended and landscaped in keeping with the attractive woodland and garden policies. Now fully operational it provides food of a very high standard within a very relaxed and informal atmopshere - bar area replete with excellent malts and decor to match the ambience of a country inn. The extended open style bistro area has been carefully planned - furnishings of a high standard with fixtures and fittings to match. Under the personal supervision of General Manager Niall Edmondson (also of Inverlochy Castle) the high standards of service prevail. Only 100 yards from the property the self catering (5 en suite rooms) Heather Cottage is situated - again quality accommodation suitably placed to take all meals (including breakfast) at the Factors Inn closeby. Whether travelling north or south this is the ideal place to pause for a couple of days (or more) and enjoy the delights of Lochaber - Ben Nevis and Bonnie Prince Charlie's monument at Glenfinnan close by. **Open to non-residents lunch and dinner**, with ample car parking.

Open: *All year*	**Swimming Pool/Health Club:** *No*
No. Rooms: *9 En Suite 9*	**Conference Facilities:** *No*
Room telephones: *Yes*	**Price Guide:** *Single £60.00*
TV in Rooms: *Yes*	*Double £95.00-£110.00*
Pets: *No* **Children:** *No*	**Location:** *3 miles north of Fort William on A82 at village*
Disabled: *Yes (one room)*	*of Torlundy*

CASTLETON HOUSE HOTEL

By Glamis, Angus, DD8 1SJ.
Tel: 01307 840340   Fax: 01307 840506
Email: hotel@castletonglamis.co.uk   www.castletonglamis.co.uk

I am delighted to report that this property continues to maintain the high standards it set last year - indeed there has been further refurbishment to some bedrooms and now there are plans to extend the hotel with further accomodation. On my last visit I was introduced to a member of the local aristocracy from Glamis (a frequent visitor) who made it quite clear how he enjoyed visiting this hotel. Praise indeed. Small but very exclusive the hotel nestles in its own grounds of garden and woodland policies amongst the gentle rolling hills of Angus not far from Glamis Castle. The 6 bedrooms are furnished and decorated to a high standard - comfort, elegance and a charm that prevails throughout the hotel. The two distinctive dining rooms (formal or the more relaxed conservatory) offer cuisine of a very high standard which I sampled myself. A mastery of culinary skills at work here with excellent technique which produces dishes of a very sound quality, clarity of flavours with a clear ambition to achieve high standards. More recognition to follow I am sure. Presentation and service could not be faulted. In addition a visit to Glamis Castle, golf at Blairgowrie only 15 minutes away could be an option. This hotel comes highly recommended - now in "safe hands" and a warm welcome is assured. 2 AA red rosettes for food. Top 200 Hotel with 3 red stars.

Open: *All year*
No. Rooms: *6 En Suite 6*
Room telephones: *Yes*
TV in Rooms: *Yes*
Pets: *Yes*   **Children:** *Yes*
Disabled: *Dining only*

Swimming Pool/Health Club: *No*
Conference Facilities: *Small - Director Level*
Price Guide: *Single £90.00 per room*
Double £120.00-£165.00 per room
Location: *A94 between Glamis and Meigle*

BOWFIELD HOTEL AND COUNTRY CLUB

Howwood, Renfrewshire PA9 1DB
Tel: 01505 705225 Fax: 01505 705230
Email: enquiries@bowfieldcountryclub.co.uk www.bowfieldcountryclub.co.uk

This hotel and country club (part of The Stonefield Castle Group) is only minutes from Glasgow airport along the A737 - out of town yet within easy reach. Situated in an attractive countryside setting the combination of the hotel and country club merge together perfectly. The hotel has 23 country style cottage bedrooms - all en suite with some nice "extra touches". The country club offers a comprehensive range of leisure and fitness facilities - also country club spa with health and beauty treatments. Swimming pool and gym popular with all club members. There are alternative menus depending on whether you require a quick snack or take dinner in the very convivial yet intimate setting of the dining room. The venue is perfect for corporate seminars or weddings. There are 17 golf courses within 25 miles - Loch Lomond within easy reach or visit the historic buildings, museums and art galleries of Glasgow. I really enjoyed my overnight stay here - staff were friendly and efficient. This hotel and country club is refreshingly different - extensive choice and the choice is yours. A very relaxed atmosphere prevalent throughout.

Open: *All year.*
No. Rooms: *23 En Suite 23*
Room telephones: *Yes*
TV in Rooms: *Yes*
Pets: *By arrangement* **Children:** *Yes*
Disabled: *Limited*

Swimming Pool/Health Club: *Yes. Country spa and beauty treatment*
Conference Facilities: *Yes*
Price Guide: *Single £80.00 (also enquire about inc. rates)*
Double £120.00
Location: *A737 from M8 at Glasgow airport. 6 mls exit Howwood (left) onto B787 and follow signs at village to Bowfield at top of the hill*

GLEDDOCH HOUSE HOTEL & COUNTRY ESTATE

Langbank, Renfrewshire PA14 6YE
Tel: 01475 540711   Fax: 01475 540201
Email: reservations@gleddochhouse.co.uk   www.gleddochhouse.co.uk

At one time the home of Sir James Lithgow, Gleddoch House Hotel commands an elevated position over the River Clyde to the hills beyond. It stands in 360 acres and is set in the peace and tranquility of the rolling Renfrewshire hills. This magnificent building contains 73 bedrooms which are furnished to a very high standard - some are quite opulent with 4 poster beds and complemented with every modern facility. Public rooms are warm and spacious which exudes peace and contentment. Recent additions have been the leisure centre with pool and a refurbishment of the club with restaurant open to non-residents. I was impressed by the friendly staff who take time to attend to your needs without being intrusive. The facilities for corporate business meetings are second to none - weddings are popular and the building and gardens lend itself to this purpose. There is an emphasis on leisure activities including clay-pigeon shoots, off road adventure driving and the equestrian centre offers guests of all ages a chance to explore the estate. The 18 hole par 72 golf course provides a unique challenge to all golfers. Only a short distance from Glasgow airport. (Please mention Stevensons when making a reservation).

Open: *All year*	**Swimming Pool/Health Club:** *Yes + beauty salon*
No. Rooms: *73 En Suite 73*	**Conference Facilities:** *Up to 150*
Room telephones: *Yes*	**Price Guide:** *Single from £99.00. Double from £150.00.*
TV in Rooms: *Yes*	**Location:** *M8 towards Greenock. Take B789*
Pets: *Yes* **Children:** *Yes*	*Langbank/Houston exit. Follow signs for ½ mile.*
Disabled: *No*	

AA⊛

HOLIDAY INN THEATRELAND

161 West Nile Street, Glasgow G1 2RL
Tel: 0141 352 8300   Fax: 0141 332 7447
email: info@higlasgow.com   www.higlasgow.com

This city centre hotel (rare experience for me) continues to uphold the high standards it set out 3 years ago when I stayed here and witnessed the complete refurbishment of the hotel. It is conveniently located next to the Royal Concert Hall and Theatre Royal and only a 5 minute walk from George Square. Ample parking closeby. The investment in this property has been massive but already owner Maurice Taylor, the well known and respected Glasgow hotelier is reaping the benefits. Management and front of house skills are exemplary. The standard, executive and penthouse suites are extremely well furnished with every modern amenity - just that extra care and attention to detail. The disabled facilities are first class. Ideal for conferences and weddings. The hotel restaurant known as "La Bonne Auberge" is the subject of an entry in my Good Food Book at the rear and takes its place as a serious player in the fine dining establishments of Glasgow. Although mainly traditional dishes there is a French influence here - à la carte casual dining or fixed menu available. Although a "modern hotel" this establishment caters for the tourist, the business traveller, the disabled and the family. General Manager : Tricia Fitzsimons.

Open: *All year*	**Swimming Pool/Health Club:** *Small gym*
No. Rooms: *113 En Suite 113*	**Conference Facilities:** *up to 100*
Room telephones: *Yes*	**Price Guide:** *Single room only tarriff (see below)*
TV in Rooms: *Yes*	*Double from £80.00-£130.00 (room only)*
Pets: *No* **Children:** *Yes*	*£180.00 (Penthouse)*
Disabled: *Yes*	**Location:** *Junction 16 (M8) Opp. Royal Concert Hall*

Scottish TOURIST BOARD ★★★★ HOTEL   AA

CASTLE HOTEL

Huntly, Aberdeenshire, AB54 4SH.
Tel: 01466 792696   Fax: 01466 792641
Email: castlehot@enterprise.net   www.castlehotel.uk.com

The investment by the Meiklejohn family in this property over the last 4 years has been immense and it is returning "to the fold" . Andrew and Linda Meiklejohn are firm in their commitment and I saw the dedication myself to return the Castle Hotel to its former glory. The former home to the Dukes of Gordon this is a magnificent 18th. century structure set in 7 acres of woodland and sweeping lawns. It lies at the heart of "the castle trail", just off the main Aberdeen to Inverness road and only a short drive from Aberdeen airport. Bedrooms (1 suite at the moment) are comfortable and spacious - most with views over the front lawn. Plans are in hand for a further 2 suites and a complete refurbishment of all bedrooms. The view from the dining room is exceptional through large windows. A separate dining venue exists for that special celebration. I was very impressed with the very friendly atmosphere here - a real effort to make sure your stay will be one from which you will return. Son Stuart and daughter Nikki take an active role with tours being organised - there is plenty to do and see. Huntly Castle (now a ruin) closeby or follow the "whisky trail". Other options could include fishing, pony trekking, golf or hillwalking.

Open: *All year ex. 25-27 December*	**Swimming Pool/Health Club:** *No*
No. Rooms: *18 En Suite 18*	**Conference Facilities:** *50+*
Room telephones: *Yes*	**Price Guide:** *Single from £48.00 - £58.00*
TV in Rooms: *Yes*	*Double from £70.00 - £110.00 (suite)*
Pets: *By arrangement* **Children:** *Yes*	**Location:** *Direct route through Huntly - follow signs*
Disabled: *Food only*	*for Huntly Castle then to Castle Hotel.*

BUNCHREW HOUSE HOTEL

Bunchrew, Inverness IV3 8TA
Tel: 01463 234917   Fax: 01463 710620
email: welcome@bunchrew-inverness.co.uk   www.bunchrew-inverness.co.uk

This magnificent , well appointed 17th. century Scottish mansion, is situated just outside Inverness on the shores of the Beauly Firth with breathtaking views of the Black Isle and Ben Wyvis to the north. It is surrounded by 20 acres of beautiful gardens and woodlands. This historic building attracts much interest and was originally built by the 8th. Lord Lovat in 1621. In April this year the hotel passed into new ownership - staff have been retained and the very high standards of the previous régime have been maintained under the very capable supervision of General Manager Gillian Omand. Head chef Walter Walker (complete with own vegetable and herb garden) takes great pride in providing traditional Scottish food - his expectations are high and there is a dedicated approach here which I have sampled myself. Well balanced combinations with clear and defined flavours. Accommodation consists of superior and standard suites, some with four poster beds and include all the "extras". Apart from the outdoor activities one associates with this area (ski-ing at Aviemore, sailing, cruising, fishing, and golf) there are a number of places of interest to visit including Culloden, Cawdor Castle and Loch Ness). AA 2 Rosettes for food. Well recommended.

Open: *All year (ex. Xmas)*	**Swimming Pool/Health Club:** *No*
No. Rooms: *14 En Suite 14*	**Conference Facilities:** *up to 80*
Room telephones: *Yes*	**Price Guide:** *Single from £90.00*
TV in Rooms: *Yes*	*Double from £145.00-£195.00*
Pets: *By arrangement* **Children:** *Yes*	**Location:** *3 miles outside city on A862 Beauly Road*
Disabled: *dining only*	

Scottish TOURIST BOARD
★★★★
SMALL HOTEL

AA ❀ ❀

THE GLENMORISTON TOWN HOUSE

Ness Bank, Inverness IV2 4SF
Tel: 01463 223777. Fax: 01463 712378
Email: glenmoriston@cali.co.uk   www.glenmoriston.com

This town house hotel was purchased this year by a local company who increased the bedroom capacity from 15 to 30 individually designed bedrooms split between two magnificent buildings. An attractive setting, just on the outskirts of the City overlooking the River Ness but only a 5 minute walk to the town centre. The fusion of the buildings here - one with the award winning La Riviera and La Terrazza restaurants - the other incorporates dedicated business facilities and rooms for private meetings, conferences and weddings. Having stayed here on two occasions I can testify to the spacious and well furnished bedrooms - many with "extras" - the cuisine enjoys an excellent reputation which has earned the hotel, amongst other accolades, 2 AA rosettes for food. Using local fresh produce it can be described as traditional Scottish cuisine with a Mediterranean influence. Most recently the Glenmoriston Town House has been chosen as the AA Courtesy and Care Award Winner for Scotland 2003-2004. The hotel has undertaken a major refurbishment in a fairly short time with emphasis on quality - front of house staff and service was excellent. It is quite clear that Glenmoriston Town House will continue to be a serious player in the hospitality industry within Inverness - indulge yourself and immerse yourself in comfort - you will enjoy your stay. Ample car parking. Highly recommended.

Open: *All year*	**Conference Facilities:** *Up to 70*
No. Rooms: *30 En Suite 30*	**Price Guide:** *Single From £85.00*
Room telephones: *Yes*	*Double From £115.00*
TV in Rooms: *Yes*	**Location:** *Ness Bank South within walking distance to City Centre*
Children: *Yes*	*AA Courtesy and Care Award for Scotland 2003-2004*
Disabled: *Dining only*	*Winner: Scottish Independent Hotel 2000*

AA ❀ ❀

JEDFOREST HOTEL AND RESTAURANT

Camptown, Jedburgh, Roxburghshire, TD8 6PJ.
Tel: 01835 840222   Fax: 01835 840226
email: info@jedforesthotel.com   www.jedforesthotel.com

This hotel has recently been purchased by Nigel & Carol Hollingworth - they have inherited this beautiful mansion house, in 35 acres of landscaped gardens with private fishing on the Jed water which flows into the river Teviot and Tweed. The previous owners had already undertaken a major refurbishment over 2 years - the bedrooms (standard to superior de luxe) have all been tastefully redecorated and furnished to a very high standard - spacious, very comfortable with magnificent views over the garden. Dining expectations are high here and I am reliably informed fully met with the appointment of a new head chef - the hotel presently holds the 2 AA rosette award for food - an indication of a high level of skills and a clear ambition to achieve high standards. The forgotten area of Scotland, this is the first and last hotel before you cross the border on the A68 - do not pass, make this your destination when travelling north or south and you will not be disappointed. This is exceptional quality combined with a very relaxed and homely atmosphere. Stay awhile - numerous historical abbeys to visit, a game of golf perhaps or a spot of fishing. Only 1 hour from Edinburgh and even less from Newcastle - a warm welcome is assured in this perfect location in the borders of Scotland. Enquire about seasonal breaks.

Open: *All Year*
No. Rooms: *12 En Suite 12*
Room telephones: *Yes*
TV in Rooms: *Yes*
Pets: *On request*   **Children:** *Over 12*
Disabled: *Yes (River Cottage)*

Swimming Pool/Health Club: *No*
Conference Facilities: *No*
Price Guide: *Single £85.00 - £125.00 (inc. dinner)*
Double £140.00 – £180.00 (inc. dinner)
B&B also available
Location: *3 miles south of Jedburgh on A68. 7 miles north of border.*

46 STEVENSONS 2004

BALLATHIE HOUSE

Kinclaven, By Stanley, Perthshire, PH1 4QN
Tel: 01250 883268   Fax: 01250 883396
Email address: email@ballathiehousehotel.com   www.ballathiehousehotel.com

Ballathie House is a short drive from Perth and situated in its own country estate setting overlooking the River Tay. The main driveway is an experience in itself with sweeping lawns and magnificent gardens stretching down to the river. This house of character dates back to 1850. The original public rooms have retained all the elegance of a country house in the true sense of the word - fine antique furnishings and period bathrooms. Premier and standard bedrooms within the main house have all been upgraded and reflect a very high quality of accommodation with all modern facilities. The sensitive development of the new riverside rooms & suites, all with views over the Tay, have proved a great success. New Sportsman's lodge rooms (en suite) and self-catering apartment available for 2004. High modern standards for fishing/sportsmen and use of all main house facilities. Priced from £45.00 per person. (Not part of grading and classification). The 2 AA red rosette award clearly demonstrates the high quality of cuisine which Ballathie is renowned for - in fact Ballathie have won many food awards - a testament to head chef Kevin MacGillivray and his team. Highly recommended and once you have visited I can assure you, you will return. AA Top 200 Hotel with 3 Red Stars. Your host at Ballathie is Chris Longden.

Open: *All year*	**Swimming Pool/Health Club:** *No*
No. Rooms: *42 En Suite 42*	**Conference Facilities:** *Boardroom meetings to 30*
Room telephones: *Yes*	**Price Guide:** *Single £79.00 Double £158.00-£220.00*
TV in Rooms: *Yes*	*2 Day breaks from £95.00 P.P.P.N., D.B.B.*
Pets: *Yes* **Children:** *Yes*	**Location:** *Off A9, 2 miles North of Perth through Stanley/or*
Disabled: *Yes*	*off A93 at Beech hedge and signs.*

AA ❀ ❀
★★★

THE FOUR SEASONS HOTEL

St. Fillans, Perthshire PH6 2NF
Tel: 01764 685333 Fax: 01764 685444
Email: info@fourseasonshotel.co.uk www.thefourseasonshotel.co.uk

Aptly named for the ever changing weather patterns, this hotel has one of the finest lochside locations in Scotland. Its position looking south west down Loch Earn must be the envy of others set amongst scenic mountains and woodland. Snugly positioned at the west end of the village the panoramic views are magnificent. "With food to match" - quote from resident proprietor Andrew Low whose experience in culinary matters are not unknown. A solid 2 AA rosette food award the kitchen was upgraded in 2002 and menus changed - one can dine formally in the Meal Reamhar Restaurant where head chef Will Thorpe demonstrates sound technical skills, harmonious and balanced combinations with sophisticated and appropriate garnishes. You can also dine in The Tarken Room - same quality but more informal. Excellent wine list to complement a good meal and finish your day with a malt around a log fire. Bedrooms are spacious and comfortable - most overlook the loch - plus 6 holiday chalets at the rear of the hotel offer more privacy. Leisure activities are too numerous to mention. The hotel can provide first class facilities for small meetings or functions and recently Andrew obtained a wedding licence for that special day. Good atmosphere here - laid back as described in the hotel brochure. Good value for money.

Open: *March - December inclusive*	**Swimming Pool/Health Club:** *No*
No. Rooms: *12 En Suite 12*	**Conference Facilities:** *Up to 36*
Room telephones: *Yes*	**Price Guide:** *Single £41.00-£74.00*
TV in Rooms: *Yes*	*Double £82.00-£98.00*
Pets: *Yes* **Children:** *Yes*	*Chalets £35.00-£70-00*
Disabled: *No*	**Location:** *A85 - west end of St. Fillans village.*

AA 🌸🌸

CAIRNBAAN HOTEL

By the Crinan Canal, Nr. Lochgilphead, Argyll PA31 8SJ
Tel: 01546 603668 Fax: 01546 606045
Email: cairnbaan.hotel@virgin.net www.cairnbaan.com

"Watch the world go by" would describe the atmosphere at The Cairnbaan Hotel. It occupies a very attractive position at the side of the Crinan Canal in this very scenic part of Argyll. Built in the late part of the 18th century it was originally a coaching inn to facilitate the building of the canal. The hotel is owned by resident proprietors Darren and Christine Dobson. During my visit I was very impressed with the high standard of accommodation – each bedroom individually designed and decorated with modern en-suite facilities. The food produce here is all locally sourced **and fresh** with scallops landed at Crinan, lobster at Ardfern, prawns from Tayvallich, haddock from Tarbert, beef from Ormsary Estate, lamb from Barbreck Estate and an abundance of wild mushrooms from the area. Culinary skills are obvious in the preparation of dishes with clarity of flavours and well balanced menus to suit all. Home made bread, pastries and associated bakery produce is the domain of Christine Dobson - Cairnbaan has an excellent reputation for morning and afternoon teas. This is a very "homely" hotel with a "hands on" situation - staff are efficient and certainly assist in creating the friendly atmosphere which prevails throughout. Places to visit include Inverary Castle, the home of The Duke of Argyll – Kilmartin Glen nearby is a favourite with lots to do and see. Less than 2 hours from Glasgow.

Open: *All year*	**Swimming Pool/Health Club:** *No*
No. Rooms: *11 En Suite 11*	**Conference Facilities:** *2 meeting rooms up to 120*
Room telephones: *Yes*	**Price Guide:** *Single £65.00 Double £85.00 to £100.00*
TV in Rooms: *Yes*	**Location:** *From Glasgow via A82 and A83 to Lochgilphead.*
Pets: *Yes* **Children:** *Yes*	*Take A816 to Cairnbaan to north of Lochgilphead.*
Disabled: *1 or 2 steps*	*(Oban Road)*

AA

INVER LODGE HOTEL

Lochinver, Sutherland IV27 4LU
Tel: 01571 844496   Fax: 01571 844395
Email: stay@inverlodge.com   www.inverlodge.com

This is a superb and modern hotel which was opened in 1988 - the quote "don't judge a book by its cover" is very apt here. The exterior of the building presents a complete contrast to its wild highland surroundings but do not be dismayed - I have stayed here for 10 consecutive years and like me you will return once you have sampled the hospitality at Inver Lodge. All 20 bedrooms and the dining room have views over Loch Inver Bay - the sunsets are spectacular. Public rooms, bedrooms and dining room are all extremely spacious and furnished to a very high standard - there are 2 suites. Executive chef, Peter Cullen displays great technical skills in the kitchen - good use of fresh local produce with a regular visit to the harbour every morning. Daily changing menu with an excellent choice of fish, meat and game. Wild mushrooms in season a speciality. It is a true testament to the General Manager Nicholas Gorton and his team that such high standards have been maintained over so many years - the service cannot be faulted - the comfort of the guest is paramount. Once you have visited Inver Lodge you will return. 3 AA Red Stars. Top 200 Hotel.

Open: *Early April-end Oct.*	**Swimming Pool/Health Club:** *Sauna*
No. Rooms: *20 En Suite 20*	**Conference Facilities:** *No*
Room telephones: *Yes*	**Price Guide:** *Single £80.00 Double from £140.00*
TV in Rooms: *Yes*	**Location:** *Through village on A835 and turn left after*
Pets: *Yes* **Children:** *Yes*	*village hall.*
Disabled: *Unsuitable*	

Scottish TOURIST BOARD ★★★★ HOTEL

AA✿
★★★

MELFORT PIER & HARBOUR

Kilmelford, by Oban, Argyll PA34 4XD
Tel: 01852 200333   Fax: 01852 200329
Email: melharbour@aol.com   www.mellowmelfort.com

Why rent a room when you can pamper yourself in the privacy of your own Luxury 5 Star Lochside house, each with its own sauna, spa bath, gourmet kitchen and underfloor heating. Most with ensuite bathrooms, log fire and laundry facilities. Some even have a sunbed. Bring your own boat and fishing equipment. Free fishing from the pier and use of a Canadian canoe and rowboat. We are open all year round and each season has its own beauty. All our houses are scattered along the rocky shores of one of the most beautiful lochs on the west coast of Scotland. Come and sit on one of our private beaches and observe the tranquility and totally unwind. Dogs and children of any age are very welcome. Dog and baby-sitting services available. The houses have 1, 2 or 3 bedrooms, all to a Scandinavian design and finished to the highest standards providing freedom, flexibility and luxury. Ideal touring base for Argyll and its many surrounding islands. Leisure activities include fishing, watersports, hill-walking and wildlife watching. Nearby horse-riding, golf, stalking, diving and great shopping. Close to cosy pubs and good restaurants. Stay two nights or a week and just relax and rejuvenate - choose the things you want to do, when you want to do them. Six of the houses are for Category 2 disabled, all on one floor and with ramps. Walk-in showers and even a sauna suitable for wheelchairs. Parking is right in front of your house.

Open: *All year (7 days a week)*	**Swimming Pool/Health Club:** *Sauna & Spa Bath in each house*
No. Houses: *15 En Suite 15 + houses*	**Conference Facilities:** *Up to 12 Director Level*
House telephones: *Yes email hook-up*	**Price Guide:** *From £75.00 – £220.00 per house/per night.*
TV in House: *Yes Satellite*	*Minimum stay 2 nights*
Pets: *2 per house* **Children:** *Yes*	**Location:** *On A816 18 miles north of Lochgilphead or 16 miles south*
Disabled: *Cat. 2. VisitScotland*	*of Oban – 1½ miles off main road. Well signposted*

Scottish
TOURIST BOARD
★★★★★
SELF
CATERING

GLENMORISTON ARMS HOTEL AND RESTAURANT

Invermoriston, by Loch Ness, Inverness-shire IV63 7YA
Tel: 01320 351206   Fax: 01320 351308
email: reception@glenmoristonarms.co.uk   www.glenmoristonarms.co.uk

A former drovers inn this property is located in the village of Invermoriston which is the gateway to the Isle of Skye and the west coast. Just a short distance from Loch Ness it enjoys an excellent geographical position midway between Inverness and Fort William. The hotel, which commands a slightly elevated position as you enter the village, is surrounded by attractive garden and woodland. The enthusiasm of new owners Nik and Hazel Hammond was quite a revelation. Already plans are in hand for a complete refurbishment of the hotel - all 8 bedrooms will be upgraded, the dining room revamped and furniture in public areas replaced to an extremely high standard. Further plans include a further 4 bedrooms and a facility for corporate meetings. Head chef Paul Lumby will have his own vegetable garden which will facilitate the AA 2 rosetted restaurant (fine dining) although bistro meals are also available. The a la carte menu offers an excellent choice of Scottish traditional cuisine. No doubt top value for money - it was like a "breath of fresh air" during my visit - a genuine highland welcome from Nik and Hazel and of course Betty MacDonald who has been here for 35 years. VisitScotland 4 stars small hotel graded.

Open: *All year except Jan & Feb*	**Swimming Pool/Health Club:** *No*
No. Rooms: *8 En Suite 8*	**Conference Facilities:** *No*
Room telephones: *Yes*	**Price Guide:** *Single £40.00-£65.00*
TV in Rooms: *Yes*	*Double £60.00-£120.00*
Pets: *No* **Children:** *Yes*	**Location:** *Midway between Inverness and Fort William*
Disabled: *No*	*on A82 - hotel in village of Invermoriston*

AA ❀ ❀

DRYBURGH ABBEY HOTEL
St. Boswell's, Melrose, Roxburghshire TD6 0RQ
Tel: 01835 822261 Fax: 01835 823945
Email: enquiries@dryburgh.co.uk www.dryburgh.co.uk

Sir Walter Scott's name is synonymous with this part of Scotland - it is also well known for fishing on the Tweed, rugby and agriculture. Just 8 miles from Melrose, in the heart of this wonderful border country, you will find Dryburgh Abbey Hotel within its own 10 acre estate of mature gardens and sweeping lawns. Views from some of the bedrooms are simply majestic - bedrooms which are furnished to a high standard, spacious and extremely comfortable. The food here is quite exceptional under the supervision of Head Chef René Gaté. (known to me from a previous régime). Whether dining in the Tweed Restaurant, overlooking the river, or merely having a snack the essence is of quality making good use of local fresh produce which is in abudance in this part of the country. The public areas (2 lounges) are creatively furnished in keeping with the style of the building offering every comfort - the swimming pool is quite luxurious and a definitive feature of the the hotel. Added to this are facilities for corporate meetings and weddings (ideal setting) - plenty of Scotland's heritage to explore here with Melrose Abbey close by (Robert The Bruce's heart lies within). Leisure activities abound - "a well rounded hotel" catering for every need. General Manager: Kevin Keenan.

Open: *All year*	**Swimming Pool/Health Club:** Yes	
No. Rooms: *38 En Suite 38*	**Conference Facilities:** *Up to 150*	
Room telephones: *Yes*	**Price Guide:** *Single £62.00*	
TV in Rooms: *Yes*	*Double £144.00 - £204.00 (superior)*	
Pets: *Yes* **Children:** *Yes*	**Location:** *At St. Boswell's turn onto A6404 and travel through*	
Disabled: *Yes (Cat 1)*	*village. 2 miles turn left onto B6356 and follow signs (2 miles).*	

WELL VIEW HOTEL

Ballplay Road, Moffat, Dumfriesshire, DG10 9JU.
Tel: 01683 220184   Fax: 01683 220088
Email: info@wellview.co.uk   www.wellview.co.uk

This is a little gem on the periphery of Moffat but within easy walking distance of the main town centre. The hotel was built in 1864 and is an imposing house of generous proportions in a wonderful garden setting with sweeping lawn to the front. Resident proprietors, Janet and John Schuckardt, have been here since 1984 and are rightly proud of their achievements - more a home than a hotel with all the comforts and food that has taken Janet to an AA 2 red rosette award (held this award for several years). Seasonal high quality ingredients used, balanced and harmonious combinations with clear, well-defined flavours. Highly acclaimed by other food critics. Bedrooms are extremely comfortable - traditional furnishings and fabrics. All has been carefully planned to convey relaxation with the warm border hospitality you receive here. The area is steeped in history - there are many places to visit including the Devil's Beef Tub, St. Mary's Loch and the border Abbeys where much of Scotland's future was settled in the early wars with England. Instead of rushing up or down the M74 take time to pay a visit to Well View Hotel. In addition to the 2 AA red rosettes has one AA red star and RAC Gold Ribbon.

Open: *All year*	**Swimming Pool/Health Club:** *No*
No. Rooms: *6 En Suite 6*	**Conference Facilities:** *Limited - 12*
Room telephones: *No*	**Price Guide:** *Single £60.00 - £70.00*
TV in Rooms: *Yes*	*Double £80.00-£112.00*
Pets: *Arrangement* **Children:** *Yes*	**Location:** *A708 from town centre, left into Ballplay Road,*
Disabled: *No*	*hotel on right.*

AA ✿ ✿

THE OPEN ARMS

Dirleton, East Lothian, EH39 5EG.
Tel: 01620 850241   Fax: 01620 850570
Email: openarms@clara.co.uk   www.openarmshotel.com

Only a short drive from Edinburgh this hotel can be found in the picturesque village of Dirleton within a short distance of the championship golf course at Muirfield. It is off the main road with very little through traffic and has one of the most beautiful village greens in Scotland. Now in the capable hands of resident owners Chris and Lyn Hansen this hotel has taken on a new lease of life - this would not have been a personal choice of mine some years ago. A "hands on" approach and a lot of hard work has taken this hotel to a new level. The Deveau Brasserie (sampled myself) in a conservatory setting is ideal for lunch or dinner overlooking Dirleton Castle or you can enjoy the more formal dining in the warm intimate restaurant. Some unusual dishes add to the enjoyment and the 1 AA red rosette award is a bench mark in itself. The 10 bedrooms have recently been upgraded - fresh and very tastefully decorated to an extremely high standard. Ideal venue for a wedding or small business meeting the balance is right here - whether on holiday, for golf or just passing through there is a very relaxed atmosphere throughout. Well recommended.

Open: *All year ex. 2 wks. Jan.*	**Swimming Pool/Health Club:** *No*
No. Rooms: *10 En Suite 10*	**Conference Facilities:** *15 board level*
Room telephones: *Yes*	**Price Guide:** *Single £85.00*
TV in Rooms: *Yes*	*Double from £130.00*
Pets: *Yes* **Children:** *Yes*	**Location:** *Between Gullane & North Berwick on*
Disabled: *Food only*	*coast road south from Edinburgh.*

CRINGLETIE HOUSE

Peebles, Peebleshire EH45 8PL
Tel: 01721 725750 Fax: 01721 725751
Email: enquiries@cringletie.com www.cringletie.com

A favourite with many a visitor to Scotland this fine baronial mansion, built in 1861, has thankfully returned to private ownership. Designed by the famous architect David Bryce it was once the home to the Wolfe Murray family. New owners, Mr. and Mrs. Van Houdt, have already initiated changes for the better but a very substantial refurbishment programme is planned well into next year. This property deserves such attention - all bedrooms and function room are being refurbished - all public areas are being upgraded and one of the very first changes already implemented was the kitchen. There is a marked improvement in the quality of cuisine and service - the kitchen walled garden with fresh fruit and vegetables a feature. The building retains its 19th. century charm with stunning views over the Moorfoot Hills. The gardens are a delight with an "all weather" tennis court. This is a fully functional country house which will soon take its rightful place as one of Scotland's leading hotels - as it was some years ago under a previous regime. Appraisal was difficult last year but I am so confident about the future of this property I have personally booked a dinner party for 12 and an overnight stay for July next year. 2 miles north of Peebles and a half hour drive to Edinburgh.

Open: *Closed Jan 8th to March 1st*	**Swimming Pool/Health Club:** *No*
No. Rooms: *14 En Suite 14*	**Conference Facilities:** *50-60*
Room telephones: *Yes*	**Price Guide:** *Single from £130.00*
TV in Rooms: *Yes*	*Double £175.00-£265.00*
Pets: *Yes* **Children:** *Yes*	**Location:** *From Peebles take A703 north –*
Disabled: *No*	*2 miles on left*

Scottish TOURIST BOARD ★★★★ SMALL HOTEL *AA* ❀ ❀

KINFAUNS CASTLE HOTEL

Near Perth, Perthshire, PH2 7JZ.
Tel: 01738 620777   Fax: 01738 620778
Email: email@kinfaunscastle.co.uk   www.kinfaunscastle.co.uk

Although dating back to the 14th. century the present castle was built in 1820 for Lord Gray by the architect Sir Robert Smirke. It is an outstanding property, located just outside Perth in majestic grounds with sweeping lawns to the front. I was witness to the renaissance of this property since it was purchased by James Smith, a Scot, who had spent many years with the Hilton International Group. The result of his efforts now place this castle hotel as one of the finest in Scotland. The heraldic theme prevails throughout - fine antique furnishings abound and the 16 bedrooms have all the elegance one would expect of a castle hotel. There are some oriental touches which add that extra interest. The cuisine is described as a blend of continental with a Scottish influence - head chef Jeremy Brazelle and his team make excellent use of Perthshire's natural larder - menus are creative and he has quickly earned a reputation for his culinary skills. The library restaurant is stunning with its spectacular marble fireplace. A number of leisure activites can be part of your itinery here - golf, horse riding, fishing or shooting could be your choice. Only a short drive from Edinburgh this is an excellent choice for your stay in Scotland. AA Top 200 Hotel with 3 Red Stars.

Open: *All year (ex. 3 wks January)*	**Swimming Pool/Health Club:** *No*
No. Rooms: *16 En Suite 16*	**Conference Facilities:** *Up to 60*
Room telephones: *Yes*	**Price Guide:** *Single £125.00 - £180.00*
TV in Rooms: *Yes*	*Double £190.00 - £320.00*
Pets: *Arrangement* **Children:** *Over 12*	**Location:** *Just outside Perth on A90 Dundee Road.*
Disabled: *Food only*	*Clearly signposted.*

KNOCKENDARROCH HOUSE

High Oakfield, Pitlochry, Perthshire PH16 5HT
Tel: 01796 473473 Fax: 01796 474068
Email: info@knockendarroch.co.uk www.knockendarroch.co.uk

An elegant Victorian mansion Knockendarroch commands breathtaking views overlooking the Tummel Valley and Pitlochry with the hills beyond. Resident proprietors Tony and Jane Ross (excellent hosts I should add) have brought a new dimension to this property over the last 7 years. The experience shows through significantly with their reinvestment in the property with quality in mind and a freshness which makes one feel quite contented in the well furnished and "homely" lounge. Jane applies all her expertise in the kitchen with dishes that are quite imaginative and cooked with a certain flair. There is an ever changing daily menu and the hotel has earned an AA red rosette in its own right. The "homely" atmosphere is reflected throughout the hotel with 12 very comfortable bedrooms - the 1½ acres of garden, although close to the town centre, gives one the necessary isolation and peace of a country house hotel. Local attractions include the Pitlochry Festival Theatre which is of international repute. For the more sport minded there are a number of activities including fishing, walking and golf. There is a policy of "no smoking" throughout the hotel.

Open: *February - November*	**Swimming Pool/Health Club:** *No*
No. Rooms: *12 En Suite 12*	**Conference Facilities:** *No*
Room telephones: *Yes*	**Price Guide:** *Single £77.00 - £95.00 (includes dinner)*
TV in Rooms: *Yes*	*Double £120.00 - £148.00 (includes dinner)*
Pets: *No* **Children:** *Over 12*	**Location:** *Proceed up Bonnethill Road from the main*
Disabled: *Unsuitable*	*road through Pitlochry and take first right.*

AA

POOL HOUSE

Poolewe, By Achnasheen, Wester Ross. IV22   2LD
Tel : 01445 781272   Fax: 01445 781403.
Email : enquiries@poolhousehotel.com   www.poolhousehotel.com

Situated close to the famous Inverewe Gardens at the head of Loch Ewe this hotel enjoys one of the most beautiful views in Wester Ross. The original house is 300 years old and formerly the home to the Mackenzies of Gairloch and Osgood Mackenzie, the founder of Inverewe Gardens. Peter and Margaret Harrison, with the able assistance of their daughters Elizabeth and Mhairi have transformed the interior of this hotel to the Victorian splendour of it's heyday - creating a standard in the highlands often hoped for but rarely found. The five large proportioned suites are absolutely magnificent in every detail - the ensuite bathrooms a real feature of a bygone era. With panoramic views over Loch Ewe this is the perfect place to indulge yourself. Chef John Moir (married to Mhairi to keep it in the family) enjoys an enviable reputation - fresh seafood in abundance with scallops from Loch Ewe a speciality. Dining here is a marvellous experience and, not before time, has been recognised by other agencies. AA Top 200 (3 red stars) achieved this year with 2 AA rosettes for food. RAC Blue Ribbon. VisitScotland 4   stars. Gold award for the Green Tourism Business Scheme. Scotland's AA Hotel of the Year 2001. A very friendly relaxed atmosphere prevails throughout and family run in the true sense of the word.

Open: *Closed Jan-Feb*	**Swimming Pool/Health Club:** *No*
No. Rooms: *5 suites*	**Conference Facilities:** *No*
Room telephones: *Yes*	**Price Guide:** *Double £220.00-£350.00 (all suites)*
TV in Rooms: *Yes*	*Seasonal breaks available.*
Pets: *No* **Children:** *Over 14*	**Location:** *Next to Inverewe Gardens.*
Disabled: *No*	

CUILLIN HILLS HOTEL

Portree, Isle of Skye, Inverness-shire IV51 9QU
Tel: 01478 612003   Fax: 01478 613092
Email: office@cuillinhills.demon.co.uk   www.cuillinhills.demon.co.uk

Built in the 1870s as a hunting lodge for Lord Macdonald of the Isles this hotel enjoys one of the finest and most spectacular views in Scotland overlooking Portree Bay and beyond. Set in fifteen acres of mature gardens the hotel has undergone a complete refurbishment programme over the last 5 years. Premier bedrooms offer that little bit of extra comfort - spacious and excellent en suite facilities with views over Portree harbour. The "courtyard" rooms (10 yards from main building) have all been fully upgraded to premier status. Plans are now in hand to upgrade standard rooms and to improve the general policies around the property which will further enhance the character of this fine hotel. Ever changing menus make good use of natural local produce including highland game, lobster, scallops and other fresh seafood. A fine dining experience here indeed - candle lit with views over the bay added to the enjoyment. Service could not be faulted. Other facilities include corporate hospitality - ideal for that board meeting and as one would expect weddings are very popular in the perfect location. The magnificent Cuillin Hills beckon. RAC Blue Ribbon. Your host is Murray McPhee.

Open: *All year*	**Swimming Pool/Health Club:** *No*
No. Rooms: *28 En Suite 28*	**Conference Facilities:** *Yes*
Room telephones: *Yes*	**Price Guide:** *Single £60.00-£85.00*
TV in Rooms: *Yes*	*Double £120.00-£220.00*
Pets: *No* **Children:** *Yes*	**Location:** *Turn right ¼ mile north of Portree on A855 and*
Disabled: *Ground floor only*	*follow signs for hotel*

Scottish TOURIST BOARD ★★★★ HOTEL **AA**

OLD MANOR COUNTRY HOUSE HOTEL

Lundin Links, Near St. Andrews, Fife KY8 6AJ
Tel: 01333 320368 Fax: 01333 320911
Email: enquiries@oldmanorhotel.co.uk   www.oldmanorhotel.co.uk

An extremely well positioned country house near the home of golf at St. Andrews. It commands extensive views over Largo Bay and Lundin Links Open qualifying golf course. The Clark family (Alistair, Dorothy and sons George and Michael) have been here for a number of years now and are known for their absolute commitment to the high standards of hospitality they maintain. A warm welcome, efficient service, comfort and cuisine of the highest calibre. Always re-investing, the Conservatory Brasserie has been a great success and the Atrium has added a new dimension near the reception area. The Brasserie (within the hotel) and Coachman's Bistro (in the grounds) are firm favourites for informal meals - uncomplicated dishes with good use of seasonal fresh produce. The fine dining area has been reduced in size - more sophisticated dishes with some innovation are reflected in the AA 2 rosette award. I knew this hotel in the 80s before the Clark family took over - there can be no comparison. The views, quality of furnishings, the 3 different dining experiences, the elegance, the warmth, combined with efficient and friendly service makes this a destination you should not miss when visiting Fife, a golfers' paradise only 45 minutes from Edinburgh.

Open: *All year.*	**Swimming Pool/Health Club:** *No*
No. Rooms: *23 En Suite 23*	**Conference Facilities:** *Up to 100.*
Room telephones: *Yes*	**Price Guide:** *Single £90.00-£110.00*
TV in Rooms: *Yes*	*Double £130.00-£200.00*
Pets: *Yes* **Children:** *Yes*	**Location:** *On A915 Kirkcaldy-St. Andrews, 1 mile east of*
Disabled: *Limited*	*Leven, on right overlooking Largo Bay.*

EDDRACHILLES HOTEL

Badcall Bay, Scourie, Sutherland IV27 4TH
Tel: 01971 502080 Fax: 01971 502477
Email: enq@eddrachilles.com www.eddrachilles.com

This hotel is superbly situated on Badcall Bay with magnificent views. This building was a former manse and has been completely refurbished providing every comfort. This is a mecca for wildlife enthusiasts with native otters, seals, roe and red deer. Handa Island nearby is a bird sanctuary and there are many small islands in the bay that can be visited by boat. The 11 en suite bedrooms are comfortably furnished, some with views over the bay. Now in their third season, Graham and Fiona Deakin demonstrate a commitment to the comfort of their guests with excellent home cooking and menus offering a varied choice. Table d'hôte or a là carte with good use of fresh natural Scottish produce locally sourced. A feature of the hotel is the sun porch which is tastefully furnished and where one can relax after dinner with coffee and liqueur. Excellent base for excursions to Durness and Cape Wrath in the north or Ullapool and The Summer Isles to the south.

Open: *March-October*	**Swimming Pool/Health Club:** *No*
No. Rooms: *11 En Suite 11*	**Conference Facilities:** *No*
Room telephones: *Yes*	**Price Guide:** *Single £45.00-£60.00 Double £90.00-£115.00*
TV in Rooms: *Yes*	**Location:** *Off A894 2 miles south of Scourie.*
Pets: *No* **Children:** *Over 3*	
Disabled: *Unsuitable*	

KILCAMB LODGE HOTEL

Strontian, Argyll, PH36 4HY.
Tel: 01967 402257   Fax: 01967 402041
Email: enquiries@kilcamblodge.com   www.kilcamblodge.com

Its position at the side of Loch Sunart on the Ardnamuchan Peninsula is spectacular with stunning views. This country house with 11 bedrooms has recently been taken over by David and Sally Fox who immediately set about taking this property to a new level with a "hands on" attitude. The bedrooms are spacious and furnished to a very high standard - most with views across the loch. Public areas offer every comfort with log fires - elegance, warmth and charm surround you at this hotel. Head Chef Neil Mellis is a master of culinary skills producing a high level of cuisine - mainly traditional but sourcing fresh seasonal produce from his own doorstep. Awarded 2 AA red rosettes for food which demonstrates a high level of dedication and technical skills. An excellent base for exploring the Peninsula or Fort William via the Corran Ferry, over to Mull also by ferry or even a trip to Skye via Mallaig (another ferry!!). Stay awhile and enjoy a very relaxed "homely" atmosphere at Kilcamb Lodge. No smoking throughout. AA top 200 hotel with 2 red stars. Highly recommended.

Open: *Closed January*	**Swimming Pool/Health Club:** *No*
No. Rooms: *11 En Suite 11*	**Conference Facilities:** *No*
Room telephones: *Yes*	**Price Guide:** *Single £70.00*
TV in Rooms: *Yes*	*Double. £110.00 - £170.00*
Pets: *Dogs welcome* **Children:** *Over 12*	**Location:** *Corran ferry 8 mls south of Ft William (A82)*
Disabled: *No*	*then 13 mls to Strontian.*

Scottish TOURIST BOARD
★★★★ SMALL HOTEL

AA ❀❀
★★

MANSFIELD HOUSE HOTEL

Scotsburn Road, Tain, Ross-Shire IV19 1PR
Tel: 01862 892052 Fax: 01862 892260
Email: info@mansfieldhouse.eu.com www.edinburghinns.eu.com

This late Victorian Mansion house built in 1905 has been upgraded over the past years to a luxury country house hotel. Recently purchased, the new owners, under the personal supervision of experienced General Manager Betty Coyle, have introduced a vitality to this property with excellent standards of hospitality. The bedrooms in the main house have been refurbished to their former glory all with en suite facilities. Features include plaster cornices and high ceilings. The master bedroom, the Haakon room, is named after the late King of Norway, who stayed in the house during the war. Its large bathroom is equipped with both a shower and a jacuzzi. The modern wing is in keeping with the surroundings and has 10 well-equipped bedrooms. Menus are interesting and varied - uncomplicated dishes of sound quality using fresh produce from the area. The 'tear-shaped' grounds are magnificent with sweeping lawns down to the entrance. There are excellent golfing facilities in the area with 8 courses to be found within a 25 mile radius including Royal Dornoch. Shooting and angling are other favourites. Tain is also the 'home' of the famous, world renowned Glenmorangie malt whisky. VisitScotland 4 star hotel rated with one AA rosette for food.

Open: *All year*	**Swimming Pool/Health Club:** *No*
No. Rooms: *18 En Suite 18*	**Conference Facilities:** *Up to 25*
Room telephones: *Yes*	**Price Guide:** *Single £65.00-£95.00*
TV in Rooms: *Yes*	*Double £110.00-£170.00 (Junior suites)*
Pets: *No* **Children:** *Yes*	**Location:***From South - 2nd turning on right from A9 (Tain Bypass).*
Disabled: *unsuitable*	*Turn left then right into Scotsburn Road. Hotel 200 metres on left.*

Scottish
TOURIST BOARD
★★★★
HOTEL

AA

STONEFIELD CASTLE HOTEL

Tarbert, Loch Fyne, Argyll PA29 6YJ
Tel: 01880 820836 Fax: 01880 820929
Email: enquiries@stonefieldcastle.co.uk www.innscotland.com

Stonefield Castle is set in 60 acres of woodland gardens that contain some of the finest Himalayan Rhododendrons and other exotic shrubs. The castle itself is a superb example of Scottish Baronial architecture built in 1837 and originally home to the Campbell family. It has retained much of its original furnishings, wood panelling, ornate ceilings and marble fireplaces alongside family portraits. Relax in the two spacious lounges or sample a pre-dinner drink in the panelled cocktail bar. Experience the very best of Scottish cuisine including shellfish, seasonal game and the famous Loch Fyne kipper. The view from the dining room over Loch Fyne is one of the best I have seen. Away from the "hustle and bustle" there are corporate facilities here for up to 150 persons and weddings are popular in such a perfect setting. Very handy overnight stay for the Islay Ferry or stay awhile and explore this wonderful part of Argyll. Recreational activities include golf, horse riding, sea and loch fishing. General Manager: Alistair Wilkie.

Open: *All year*	**Swimming Pool/Health Club:** *No*
No. Rooms: *33 En Suite 33*	**Conference Facilities:** *Yes*
Room telephones: *Yes*	**Price Guide:** *Single £90.00-£100.00*
TV in Rooms: *Yes*	*Double £180.00-£250.00 (suites)*
YesNo **Children:** *Yes*	**Location:** *From Lochgilpead take Tarbert Road (A83)*
Disabled: *Limited*	*south for 10 miles.*

FORSS COUNTRY HOUSE HOTEL

Forss, By Thurso, Caithness KW14 7XY
Tel: 01847 861201/202 Fax: 01847 861301
Email: jamie@forsshouse.freeserve.co.uk   www.forsscountryhouse.co.uk

Only 4 miles from Thurso on the A836 you will find Forss Country House Hotel nestling in 20 acres of woodland beside a picturesque water mill. Over the years Jamie and Jackie MacGregor have refurbished this hotel and introduced standards which have merited a VisitScotland 4 star assessment. Many of my hotel entries are small friendly independently family run establishments and this is no exception with excellent "all round" hospitality. An extensive choice of quality wines compliments dishes from locally caught fish, local beef, lamb and fresh vegetables in season. In addition to the well proportioned bedrooms within the hotel – all with modern en suite facilities there are 5 sportsmens lodges with all the comforts one would expect in the well maintained grounds. There is a very comfortable cocktail bar with almost 300 malts and lounge with log fire. Only 15 minutes away is the Scottish "home" of the late Queen Mother, the Castle of Mey, which is now open to the public. Not far from John O'Groats, convenient for a day trip to the Orkney Islands.

Open: *All year (closed 23rd Dec – 5th Jan)*	**Disabled:** *Limited*
No. Rooms: *13 En Suite 13*	**Swimming Pool/Health Club:** *No*
Room telephones: *Yes*	**Conference Facilities:** *Up to 30*
TV in Rooms: *Yes*	**Price Guide:** *Single £60.00*
Pets: *Yes* **Children:** *Yes*	*Double £95.00*
	Location: *4 miles from Thurso on A836*

HIGHLAND COTTAGE

Breadalbane Street, Tobermory, Isle of Mull, Argyll PA75 6PD

Tel: 01688 302030

Email: davidandjo@highlandcottage.co.uk   www.highlandcottage.co.uk

Since my visit and overnight stay this property has now achieved AA Top 200 status. This category was introduced last year to recognise the top 200 hotels in the UK. Highland Cottage is a small converted street cottage overlooking Tobermory Bay and a gem of a place to find in Tobermory - well away from the main tourist activity with solace and tranquility on offer. The building has been renovated from scratch and extends to every requirement for the discerning traveller. Bedrooms are all carefully furnished with antiques, named after Scottish islands and some with four poster beds - found to be immaculate indeed. David & Jo Currie, resident proprietors, are to be complemented on attention to detail but retain a very relaxed, homely atmosphere. I can only describe the food as excellent. Jo's culinary skills are quite exceptional - taste, texture, good use of fresh produce and presentation could not be faulted. Coffee in the conservatory was the perfect ending to the day. There is so much to see and visit on Mull including a trip to Iona, a visit to Duart Castle (home of the MacLean Chief) or whatever you fancy. I would advise a three day stay or more when visiting Mull and Highland Cottage. RAC Blue Ribbon and AA Top 200 hotel with 2 red stars.

Open: *All year ex. Mid Oct-Mid Nov Restricted Opening Jan-Feb*	**Swimming Pool/Health Club:** *No*
No. Rooms: *6 En Suite 6*	**Conference Facilities:** *Small board meetings*
Room telephones: *Yes*	**Price Guide:** *Single from £75.00 Double from £99.00 Dinner £28.50*
TV in Rooms: *Yes*	
Pets: *Yes* **Children:** *Over 8*	**Location:** *Roundabout at top of town – straight across then first right into Breadalbane Street*
Disabled: *Yes Cat. 1 STB*	

Scottish TOURIST BOARD ★★★★ SMALL HOTEL   **AA** ❀ ❀ ★★

LOCH TORRIDON COUNTRY HOUSE HOTEL

Torridon, Wester Ross IV22 2EY
Tel: 01445 791242 Fax: 01445 791296
Email: enquiries@lochtorridonhotel.com www.lochtorridonhotel.com

This property is well known to me and commands an exceptional position amongst 58 acres of rugged mountain scenery overlooking Loch Torridon. Originally built in 1887 it was owned by the Earl of Lovelace and was a Victorian shooting lodge in the grand style of the day. The ornate ceilings and wood panelled public areas are a feature. Now in private hands as a country house hotel the grand style of a bygone era continues today - the 19 bedrooms (some recently refurbished) range from standard through superior, deluxe and master with magnificent en suite bathrooms. The dedicated approach of executive chef Kevin J Broome is evident here - quality ingredients sourced locally as one would expect - an abundance of natural larder on your own doorstep. Open all year except 3 weeks in January; check out the very attractive winter breaks - this is the "great outdoors" here with a host of leisure activities to hand - or just enjoy the peace and contentment with a good book. The hotel is now owned and managed by Daniel & Rohaise (née Gregory) Rose-Bristow with David & Geraldine Gregory enjoying their retirement. AA top 200 hotel with 3 red stars and 2 AA red rosettes for food. Inverness - 65 miles.

Open: *All year ex. 3 weeks January*	**Swimming Pool/Health Club:** *No*
No. Rooms: *19 En Suite 19*	**Conference Facilities:** *16 Director level*
Room telephones: *Yes*	**Price Guide:** *Single £60.00-£104.00*
TV in Rooms: *Yes*	*Double £97.00-£315.00 (master room rates)*
Pets: *No* **Children:** *Yes*	**Location:** *Inverness - Achnasheen. Take A832 to Kinlochewe*
Disabled: *Yes*	*village. Take turning clearly marked Torridon 10 miles.*

Scottish TOURIST BOARD ★★★★ HOTEL

AA ❀❀
★★★

SHARROW BAY COUNTRY HOUSE

Lake Ullswater, Penrith, Cumbria CA10 2LZ
Tel: 017684 86301 or 017684 86483   Fax: 017684 86349

email: enquiries@sharrow-bay.com   www.sharrow-bay.com

The names of the late Francis Coulson MBE and Brian Sack MBE are synonymous with the highest traditions of hotel keeping. Nigel Lightburn, formerly Managing Director, has maintained these fine traditions - there have been innovations and some changes to "move with the times" which have been welcomed. The elder statesmen of the prestigious Relais & Chateaux in the UK (37th year) and now an AA Top 200 hotel (UK) it offers every comfort for the discerning traveller. Built in 1840 Sharrow Bay Country House commands breathtaking views over Lake Ullswater and is the perfect retreat in all aspects. My fourth overnight stay in April was as enjoyable as ever - outstanding cuisine and accommodation to match - you have to book well in advance for the popular garden suites. Exciting plans are well advanced which will increase the facilities at this property and appeal to a wider age group but still maintain the quality that Sharrow Bay is renowned for - previous winner of the Harpers International Wine competition, Decanter magazine award for excellence, AA 3 red rosettes for food and the RAC Gold Ribbon Award. Within easy reach of Scotland going north and return when travelling south. Highly recommended.

Open: *March - December*	**Swimming Pool/Health Club:** *No*
No. Rooms: *25 En Suite 22*	**Conference Facilities:** *Yes - up to 20*
Room telephones: *Yes*	**Price Guide:** *Single £140.00 (includes dinner)*
TV in Rooms: *Yes*	*Double £300.00-£420.00 (includes dinner)*
Pets: *No* **Children:** *Over 13*	**Location:** *M6 - exit 40 - A66 west - A592 Pooley Bridge,*
Disabled: *Yes*	*turn right after church*

MARLFIELD HOUSE

Gorey, Co. Wexford, Ireland.
Tel: 353 (0)55 21124   Fax: 353 (0)55 21572
Email: info@marlfieldhouse.ie   www.marlfieldhouse.com

Once again I am delighted to include Marlfield House as my Irish "Associate Hotel" for edition 2004. It came strongly recommended and is a member of the prestigous Relais & Chateaux group. Formerly the residence of the Earls of Courtown Marlfield House is a very elegant 19th. century mansion set in its own grounds of wonderful garden, woodland and parkland policies. The State Rooms are decorated with rich fabrics and fine antique furniture - all have period marble fireplaces and elegant marble bathrooms. Every room is spacious and offers every luxury. The interior of the hotel is resplendent with fine paintings and antiques and the conservatory is a feature overlooking the garden. Modern Irish cuisine here which has been awarded 3 AA red rosettes for food. The Bowe family are to be congratulated on keeping the standards of yesterday today. To maintain such high standards is testament to a firm commitment and dedication. Relais & Chateaux members since 1984 Marlfield House has an AA top 200 (UK and Ireland) rating with 3 red stars and an RAC Gold Ribbon award. General Manager: Margaret Bowe.

Open: *Feruary - mid December*	**Swimming Pool/Health Club:** *No*
No. Rooms: *13 (6 suites) En Suite 13*	**Conference Facilities:** *Small - Director Level*
Room telephones: *Yes*	**Price Guide:** *Double. Room - Standard:* ***Euro 235-255***
TV in Rooms: *Yes*	*State Rooms:* ***Euro 425-730***
Pets: *Arrangement* **Children:** *Yes*	**Location:** *80 km south of Dublin*
Disabled: *Not suitable*	

AA 🌐🌐🌐
★★★

YNYSHIR HALL

Eglwysfach, Machynlleth, Powys, SY20 8TA
Tel: 01654 781209   Fax: 01654 781366

email: info@ynyshir-hall.co.uk   www.ynyshir-hall.co.uk

A recent addition to the prestigous Relais & Chateaux (2002) this country house property upholds the finest traditions of hotel keeping. Opulence and gracious living on a fine scale. This beautiful country retreat (a 16th. century manor) is surrounded by magnificent gardens and could be described as the perfect "hideaway" to indulge yourself. The 9 bedrooms which include 2 suites are perfectly appointed - large with antique beds and furniture to complement. Owners Rob and Joan Reen have used their immense talents (Rob is an artist) to create interiors which express warmth, elegance and charm. The AA 3 red rosette award for food demonstrates a high commitment in achieving high standards of cuisine using high quality suppliers with fresh seasonal produce. Excellent technical skills successfully executed. Cocktail bar with log fire and restaurant with fine linen and glassware allied with an excellent wine list is the complete dining experience. Ideal location for a visit to the Dovey estuary - one of the finest bird reserves in the country. AA top 200 hotel (UK) with 3 red stars. RAC Gold Ribbon and 5 stars from the Welsh Tourist Board.

Open: *All year ex. 5th-25th Jan.*	**Swimming Pool/Health Club:** *No*
No. Rooms: *9 (2 suites) En Suite 9*	**Conference Facilities:** *Director level 25*
Room telephones: *Yes*	**Price Guide:** *Single £95.00 - £180.00*
TV in Rooms: *Yes*	*Double £125.00-£215.00 Suites £250.00 - £275.00*
Pets: 1 room only **Children:** *Over 9*	**Location:** *10 miles from Aberwystwyth.*
Disabled: *unsuitable*	

THE OLD SMIDDY GUEST HOUSE

Laide, Gairloch, Wester Ross IV22 2NB
Tel: 01445 731425 Fax: 01445 731696
Email: oldsmiddy@aol.com www.oldsmiddy.co.uk

Previously an entry in my **Good Food Book** there will be some dismay that Kate Macdonald has now reverted to Bed & Breakfast only. She had built up an envious reputation, however - don't forget her national award winning breakfast, utilising the finest of Scotland's larder and complimented by her superb home baking. Just a few miles north of Gairloch and not far from Inverewe Gardens the Old Smiddy is a cottage style guest house - well tended gardens with views over the hills add to the attraction. The 3 bedrooms are comfortably furnished with extra "touches" and one superior room has direct access from a patio to the garden. If you are looking for peace and quiet, wide open spaces with dramatic breathtaking views almost round every corner then Wester Ross is the place to be - there are long almost empty beaches, hill and lowland walks and excellent loch fishing. Having stayed here myself I can certainly recommend this establishment located just outside the village of Laide. In addition, there are 3 self-catering cottages which are ideal for a family or more privacy. There is a terrific ambience here. For those who use Bed & Breakfast accommodation on a regular basis you would have to go far to find a place better than this - Kate will provide the necessary information for dinner requirements. Reports please.

Open: *January - November*	**Disabled**:	*Not suitable*
No. Rooms: *3 (2 en suite & 1 private fac)*	**Smoking:**	*No smoking throughout*
Room telephones: *No*	**Covers:**	*Residents only*
TV in Rooms: *Yes*	**Price Guide:**	*£35.00 - £45.00*
Pets:	**Location:**	*15 miles north of Gairloch on main A832.*
Children: *Over 16*		

STEVENSONS

SCOTLAND'S
GOOD FOOD BOOK WITH RECIPES
2004

Photo by kind permission of The Crynoch of Lairhillock

STEVENSONS

SCOTLAND'S GOOD FOOD BOOK 2004

FOREWORD

After 20 years in this beautiful country, I am probably more Scottish than German. One of my loves of this country is the huge abundance and choice of quality ingredients that it offers (although my Scottish wife also merits a mention).

Particularly close to my heart is a desire to support and promote local suppliers and I find it disheartening to see that numerous hotel and restaurant chains insist on using national nominated suppliers. One of the key philosophies in my restaurant is to source all ingredients (as far as is possible) within a 20-mile radius. Not only do I feel that I am supporting the local economy, but I also feel that by developing a personal relationship with my suppliers, we have a better understanding of each other's needs. From this symbiotic relationship the restaurant and the customers can only benefit. It is encouraging to see that so many others in this book share my philosophy and that Alan Stevenson has successfully captured the essence of good food and Scottish hospitality, where good food is the main ingredient.

Hermann Schmid

Hermann Schmid Of 'The Crynoch At Lairhillock', Netherley, Aberdeenshire

Hermann Schmid
The Crynoch at Lairhillock

Scottish quality salmon

Quality Approved
SCOTTISH
SALMON

Fresh from the loch

www.scottishsalmon.co.uk

THE CRYNOCH AT LAIRHILLOCK

Netherley, South of Aberdeen, Aberdeen AB39 3QS
Tel: 01569 730001 Fax: 01569 731175
Email: lairhillock@breathemail.net www.lairhillock.co.uk

The Lairhillock Inn and Crynoch Restaurant date back over 250 years as an old coaching inn situated on the main drovers road between Aberdeen and Stonehaven. Owners Roger and Angela Thorne, whilst introducing modern measures to complement the existing enviable reputation, have endeavoured to retain the rustic charm and country ambiance. The head chef, Hermann Schmid, has set high standards and promotes innovative and expansive menus and this is clearly reflected by the dining experience in the Crynoch Restaurant. Dishes could include venison with chanterelles, sea bass and langoustine tails, smoked lamb, salmon risotto plus a selection of twelve different cheeses from an award winning cheese table. Fresh ingredients, sourced locally, ensure the quality and consistency of the menu. The Crynoch has been regularly voted the best restaurant in the North East and deservedly so. This country haven is not to be missed!

Open: *All Year ex. Tues. 25/26 Dec. 1/2 Jan.*	**Covers:** *Restaurant 60. Bar Meals 100*
No Rooms: *N/A*	**Price Guide:** *Lunch £13.95 Dinner from £25.00.*
TV in Rooms: *N/A* **Room Tel.** *N/A*	**Location:** *A90 south from Aberdeen to Portlethen ½ mile south*
Children: *Yes*	*turn right signposted for Durris. Follow road 3 mls*
Disabled: *Yes* **Smoking:** *Yes*	*– restaurant 300 yds. (signposted)*

ANDREW FAIRLIE@GLENEAGLES

The Gleneagles Hotel, Auchterarder, Perthshire PH3 1NF
Tel: 01764 694267 Fax: 01764 694163.
email: andrew.fairlie@gleneagles.com

Once again, my visit to this establishment this year was a gourmet delight - a very successful operation since Andrew moved from One Devonshire Gardens to Gleneagles over 2 years ago. Known by reputation he displays a passion for food and is driven by innovation, evolving ideas and concepts, with an element of excitement and daring. Technical skills are obvious in traditional or modern dishes with a consistency throughout - accurate and vibrant flavours. The importance of team work is vital states Andrew - he moved his team from Glasgow and Dale Dewsbury (General Manager) works miracles with the front of house operation. Ambience and service could not be faulted. Sophisticated wine list. Options of a la carte or tasting menu. Excellent cheese board. This is one for the connoisseur - the complete dining experience. **Scottish chef of the year 2002. AA restaurant of the year 2002 - Scotland & Northern Ireland.**

Open: *All year (Dinner only) ex 3wks Jan. Closed Sun.*	**Smoking:** *Designated area.*
No Rooms: *N/A*	**Covers:** *40*
TV in Rooms: *N/A* **Room Tel.** *N/A*	**Price Guide:** **£55.00 - £75.00**
Children: *Over 12*	*Cheese* **£12.00** *Coffee* **£5.00**
Disabled: *Unsuitable*	**Location:** *Ground floor of Gleneagles Hotel.*

JOHNSONS RESTAURANT WITH ROOMS
Braemar Road, Ballater, Royal Deeside AB35 5RQ
Tel/Fax: 01339 755762
email: info@auldkirkhotel.com   www.auldkirkhotel.com

Formerly the Auld Kirk Hotel it has recently been re-classified by VisitScotland as a "Restaurant With Rooms". It is easily located on the main road (west side) in the very attractive village of Ballater on Royal Deeside. The interior of this fine church (Kirk) building has been transformed over the last 3 years by family owners George Inglis, James and Gillian Johnson. Together they have created a culinary paradise with 7 excellent en suite rooms. Several visits and a fine dining experience convinced me that chef/patron James Johnson displays a mastery of techniques producing dishes of a very sound quality, clarity of flavours and good use of fresh ingredients. Seafood platter, Deeside river salmon and summer berry pudding could be your choice but menus offer a varied choice of meat, game and fish - well balanced and harmonious combinations. Option of a lighter meal can be taken in the comfortable lounge. Service was exemplary. There are clearly aspirations here to forge ahead and create even higher standards. Keep this one in mind during your travels. Great ambience. Reports please.

Open: *All year ex. 25,26,27 Dec. and 1,2,3 Jan.*	**Price Guide:** *Lunch £10.00-£15.00*
No Rooms: *7 en suite*	*Dinner £20.00-£32.00*
TV in Rooms: *Yes* **Room Tel:**	*Rooms: single (B&B) £55.00*
Yes	*Double (B&B) £70.00*
Children: *Yes* **Disabled:** *Dining only* **Location:** *Main road (A930 500yards west of village centre.*	

CHANCELLOR'S
Shieldhill Castle, Quothquan, Biggar, ML12 6NA
Tel: 01899 220035   Fax: 01899 221092
email: enquiries@shieldhill.co.uk www.shieldhill.co.uk

This is an outstanding restaurant within Shieldhill Castle which is steeped in history dating back to the 16th. century. The period furnishings, high ornate ceilings and large windows create the perfect ambience not to mention the award winning cuisine of head chef Ashley Gallant. The diner's high expectations are fully met with consistency throughout - demonstrates a clear ambition to achieve high standards. Good use of fresh, seasonal, high quality ingredients. Menus are really creative (just that something different which shows innovation) and the wine list must surely be one of the best in Scotland (if not the UK). Recognition by the prestigious Harpers International Wine Magazine speaks volumes. Service and attention to detail were exemplary. 2 AA red rosettes for food. Yours hosts: Christina and Bob Lamb. ***AA***

Open: *All year*	**Smoking:** *Not in restaurant*
No Rooms: *16*	**Covers:** *40*
TV in Rooms: *Yes* **Room Tel.** *Yes*	**Price Guide:** *Lunch from £14.50 (a là carte available)*
Children: *Yes*	*Dinner From £14.50 (a là carte available)*
Disabled: *Food only*	**Location:** *A702 to B7106 at Biggar to Carnworth road. 2 miles turn left and castle on right.*

THE LOFT RESTAURANT

Golf Course Road, Blair Atholl, Perthshire PH18 5TE
Tel: 01796 481377   Fax: 01796 481511
email: danny@rivertilt.fsnet.co.uk   www.theloftrestaurant.co.uk

I have been visiting this restaurant for many years now. It is clearly signposted and located just off the main street. It forms the upper part of premises which you reach through a stable door and up some stairs. Stone walls, beams and oak floor generate an atmosphere of well being - formerly a Junior Master Chef Finalist, Daniel Richardson is head chef and only 18 years old - I have known him since he was an eleven year old assisting in the kitchen. A talent already recognised as a "bright star" of the future in various food journals his commitment in the kitchen is complete dedication. Menus offer a varied choice but there is clear ambition here to achieve high standards with evidence of innovation and consistency. There is also the option to dine more informally in the conservatory bar (bistro) with menu offering adequate choice (still the quality is maintained!) and very popular with families. Service was excellent. Although Blair Atholl is now bypassed by the A9, take a pause in your travels to visit this restaurant.

Open: *All year (restricted in winter)*	**Conference Facilities:** *N/A*
No Rooms: *N/A*	**Price Guide:** *Lunch £8.50-£15.00 Dinner £15.00-£25.00*
TV in Rooms: *N/A* **Room Tel.** *N/A*	**Location:** *5 mls north of Pitlochry on A9 take B8079 to*
Pets: *N/A* **Children:** *Yes*	*Blair Atholl. 50 yds from centre of village down Golf*
Disabled: *No*	*Course Road.*

11 PARK AVENUE RESTAURANT

11 Park Avenue, Carnoustie, Angus. DD7 7JA.
Tel/Fax: 01241 853336
email: parkavenue@02.co.uk   www.11parkavenue.co.uk

This restaurant is located in the heart of Carnoustie just minutes from the championship golf course and railway station. It came to my notice through recommendation and press reports. Chef/proprietor Stephen Collinson retains a low profile and although known locally for his skills he now has a wider "audience" since I first visited in 1999. Tastefully furnished with comfortable floor plan to facilitate 50 covers Stephen applies his trade with great diligence and takes pride in his preparation. There is excellent use of natural fresh produce from land and sea. Dishes include Skye scallops, sea bass, duck confit in a chilli and lime sauce, prime fillet of Angus beef and other dishes of a more modern/classical flavour. The restaurant is open for dinner Tuesday to Saturday - lunch on Friday only. Reservations are advised. One AA red rosette award. Make a note of this one - well worth the visit. **AA**❀

Open: *All year ex. Sun/Mon + 2wks Jan.*	**Smoking:** *Restricted*
Lunch Friday only	**Covers:** *50*
No Rooms: *N/A*	**Price Guide:** *Dinner £27.00-£30.00*
	Lunch (Friday only) £15.00 - £20.00
TV in Rooms: *N/A* **Room Tel.** *N/A*	**Location:** *500 yds from railway station and 5 mins from*
Children: *Yes* **Disabled:** *Yes*	*Carnoustie golf course in centre of town.*

THE DINING ROOM

Coul House Hotel, Contin, By Strathpeffer, Ross-shire IV14 9ES

Tel: 01997 421487 Fax: 01997 421945

email: info@coulhousehotel.com   www.coulhousehotel.com

This restaurant, unusually but simply called The Dining Room is driven by newly arrived resident proprietors Stuart & Susannah Macpherson. (family are well known local hotel owners from the past) Early reports indicated that the priority was an exciting dining experience and indeed Stuart brought Executive Chef Garry Kenley (Inverness bred) from the USA where he had been working for him for the past 6 years. His classical French apprenticeship was spent with the famous BTH hotels - his passion is modern cuisine with a French influence but he is equally relaxed with traditional Scottish fayre with some innovation. Ambition here clearly to achieve high standards. Thoroughly enjoyed my meal - menus offer a varied choice (a la carte) and service was very good. Plans are well advanced to reburbish the restaurant (and the hotel) during the Winter months but expectation is high and next year further developments will be in place. No doubt further recognition from other agencies will follow. Reports please. (Please mention Stevensons when making dinner reservations).

Open: *All year*		**Smoking:**	*Designated lounge*	
No Rooms: 20		**Covers:**	*32*	
TV in Rooms: *Yes*		**Price Guide:**	*Lunch £7.50 - £15.00*	
Room Tel. *Yes*			*Dinner £23.00 - £28.00 (a la carte)*	
Children: *Yes*	**Disabled:** *Yes*	**Location:**	*A835 to Contin - 17 mls west of Inverness.*	

THE PEAT INN

Near Cupar, Fife KY15 5LH

Tel: 01334 840206 Fax: 01334 840530

Email: reception@thepeatinn.co.uk www.thepeatinn.co.uk

My appreciation for "services" to the Scottish hospitality industry this year is David Wilson (see page 1). A "well kent face" he requires no introduction and welcomes any chance to promote Scotland – in this case the abundance of natural food ingredients on our doorstep and more importantly what we do with them. David extols all that is good in Scottish Cuisine preparing dishes of outstanding quality using regional produce from the arable rich area of Fife. He has built up a world-wide reputation and since he first opened his accolades include Chef Laureate (1986) and Master Chef of Great Britain among many others. In addition to his creative à la carte menu and table d'hôte menus David offers a tasting menu of 7 courses. His interest in wines is well known. There are 8 luxury bedrooms with sitting rooms and all facilities to the rear of the inn. A great endorsement and ambassador for Scotland. AA Top 200 ★★ and 3 food Rosettes. *AA* ❀ ❀ ❀

Open: *All year except Sun/Mon,*	**Disabled:** *Yes (phone first)*	
Xmas Day & New Year's Day	**Smoking:** *No smoking in dining room*	
No Rooms: *8 En Suite*	**Covers:** *48*	
TV in Rooms: *Yes* **Room Tel.** *Yes*	**Price Guide:** *Lunch £19.50 Dinner £30-£45*	
Children: *Yes*	*Please enquire DB&B rates*	
	Location: *6 miles s.west of St.Andrews after junction of B940/941.*	

BRAIDWOODS

Drumastle Mill Cottage, By Dalry, Ayrshire KA24 4LN
Tel: 01294 833544 Fax: 01294 833553
email: keithbraidwood@btconnect.com www.braidwoods.co.uk

I knew Keith Braidwood when he was making a name for himself at Shieldhill Castle near Biggar. Part of his earlier years were spent at Inverlochy Castle in the highlands. Always with the idea that he wanted his own restaurant he chose a country cottage just outside Dalry which conveys a distinct feeling of being "in the middle of nowhere" surrounded by fields. Perfect. I have sampled Keith's culinary skills - by repute expectations of the kitchen are high and I was not disappointed. High technical skills here with flair and a consistency throughout the meal - depth and flavour evident. Restricted menu? Not so - balanced menus (lunch & dinner) offer excellent choice. Whole roast boneless quail stuffed with black pudding my favourite. Nicola's front of house skills are exemplary and always a warm welcome. AA 2 red rosette award for food. No smoking policy throughout. **AA**🏵 🏵

Open: *All year ex 3wks Jan & 2wks Sept Closed Sun dinner, Mon all day, Tues lunch*	**Covers:** *24*
Children: *Over 12*	**Price Guide:** *Lunch £16.00-£19.00 (2 or 3 Course)*
Disabled: *Not suitable*	*Dinner £32.00-£36.00 (3 or 4 course)*
Smoking: *No*	*Sunday lunch £25.00*
	Location: *Take road to Salcoats from A737 - 1 mile and follow signs.*

HALDANES RESTAURANT

39a Albany Street, Edinburgh, EH1 3QY
Tel: 0131 556 8407 Fax: 0131 556 2662
email: dinehaldanes@aol.com www.haldanesrestaurant.com

I knew chef/proprietor George Kelso 11 years ago when he worked in a country house hotel in the north of Scotland. From a difficult start and a lot of hard work Haldanes is now a serious player on the Edinburgh restaurant scene - a basement restaurant with a terrific atmosphere there is no lack of sophistication here. Comfy sofas for the pre-dinner drink (with excellent wine list) and a restaurant with great ambience. Scottish traditional produce (quality suppliers) is cooked to perfection but with an innovative style - there are clear, well defined flavours with great texture and taste. Good use of seasonal fresh produce as one would expect. À la carte menu offers an excellent range of dish (6 main) - baked monkfish & prime scottish beef a favourite. Reviews have been very complimentary and quite rightly takes its place in The Good Food Book. Situated not far from the new "Harvey Nicks" (down the hill thank goodness!) it will receive further recognition. AA 2 red rosette food award. **AA**🏵 🏵

Open: *All year 25th/26th Dec.*	**Smoking:** *Designated area*
No Rooms: *N/A*	**Covers:** *48*
TV in Rooms: *N/A* **Room Tel.** *N/A*	**Price Guide:** *Lunch £12.00-£18.00*
Children: *Yes*	*Dinner £25.00-£35.00 (Min £15.00)*
Disabled: *No*	**Location:** *New Town - cnr. Albany St/York Lane just down from the new "Harvey Nicks" & St Andrew's Sq*

IGGS RESTAURANT

15 Jeffrey Street, Edinburgh EH1 1DR
Tel: 0131 557 8184 Fax: 0131 652 3774
email: iggsbarioja@aol.com

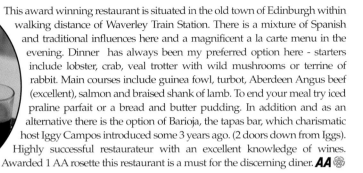

This award winning restaurant is situated in the old town of Edinburgh within walking distance of Waverley Train Station. There is a mixture of Spanish and traditional influences here and a magnificent a la carte menu in the evening. Dinner has always been my preferred option here - starters include lobster, crab, veal trotter with wild mushrooms or terrine of rabbit. Main courses include guinea fowl, turbot, Aberdeen Angus beef (excellent), salmon and braised shank of lamb. To end your meal try iced praline parfait or a bread and butter pudding. In addition and as an alternative there is the option of Barioja, the tapas bar, which charismatic host Iggy Campos introduced some 3 years ago. (2 doors down from Iggs). Highly successful restaurateur with an excellent knowledge of wines. Awarded 1 AA rosette this restaurant is a must for the discerning diner. **AA** ❀

Open: *All year (Sunday closed)*	**Smoking:** *Yes*
No Rooms: *N/A*	**Covers:** *60*
TV in Rooms: *N/A* **Room Tel.** *N/A*	**Price Guide:** *Lunch £12.50-£15.00*
Children: *Yes*	*Dinner £25.00-£30.00*
Disabled: *Yes*	**Location:** *Between Royal Mile and Market Street behind Waverley Station and John Knox's House.*

MARTINS RESTAURANT

70 Rose Street North Lane, Edinburgh EH2 3DX
Tel: 0131 225 3106 Fax: 0131 220 3403
Email: mirons@fsbdial.co.uk

For many years now Martins has been regarded as one of the finest restaurants in Edinburgh. It is discreetly situated between Frederick / Castle Street in the north lane of Rose Street. The secret of this establishment is the consistently high standards set by Martin & Gay Irons since 1983 allied with the knowledge of sourcing good food - most of the suppliers are known on a personal level. Once inside you will experience the perfect ambience - a relaxed atmosphere with exceptional personal attention and cuisine, carefully prepared that reflects a high quality of culinary skills. Dishes include chargrilled rabbit with wild mushrooms, seared fillet of sea bass, seared scallops with spinach, wild Scottish salmon and roast loin of lamb all prepared with great care - excellent use of wild ingredients. Renowned for his cheeseboard Martin can advise accordingly. The perfect gourmet experience. AA 2 red rosetted restaurant. **AA** ❀ ❀

Open: *All year except 23 Dec-16 Jan*	**Smoking:** *No smoking in dining areas*
24 May-4 June & 25 Sept-6 Oct	**Covers:** *36+ Private Dining*
No Rooms: *N/A*	**Price Guide:** *Lunch from £12.50 Dinner £30-£36.00*
TV in Rooms: *N/A* **Room Tel.** *N/A*	**Location:** *North Lane off Rose Street between Frederick and*
Children: *No* **Disabled:** *Unsuitable*	*Castle Street.*

NUMBER ONE RESTAURANT
1, Princes Street, Edinburgh EH2 2EQ
Tel : 0131 557 6727   Fax : 0131 557 3747
email : numberone@thebalmoralhotel.com   www.rfhotels.com

In keeping with the fine traditions of The Good Food Book this restaurant rightfully takes its place amongst the others included in my personal choice. Although part of the Balmoral Hotel the restaurant has created a reputation in its own right for fine dining - executive chef Jeff Bland whose culinary expertise is well known displays a quality of skills which have brought him recognition from many agencies and a number of awards. Jeff is equally at home with modern or traditional dishes - good combinations showing flair and imagination. High technical skills with some innovation, good texture and taste. There is a depth to the cusine here which is apparent throughout the meal. There can be no doubt that diners expectations are fully realised - also a fine wine list available for the connoisseur. Ambience perfect with fine furnishings and white linen - sound advice and service impeccable. Restaurant Manager: Gary Quinn. **AA**❀ ❀

Open: *Closed first week January*	**Smoking:** *Restricted*
No Rooms: *N/A*	**Covers:** *50*
TV in Rooms: *N/A* **Room Tel.** *N/A*	**Price Guide:** *Lunch from £15.00-£25.00 Dinner £41.00*
Children:*Yes*	*(also à la carte)*
Disabled: *Lift through kitchen*	**Location:** *East end of Princes Street*

THE BUTTERY
652 Argyle Street, Glasgow G3 8UF
Tel: 0141 221 8188   Fax: 0141 204 4639
email: ia.fleming@btopenworld.com

Established in 1869, this is Glasgow's oldest and most celebrated restaurant. Stained glass doors lead you past the impressive mahogany and marble bar into the unique wood-panelled dining room. Owner Ian Fleming and Executive Chef Willie Deans form a formidable team renowned for their management and culinary skills. The decor has been "toned down" a bit from the Victorian image but still retains the elegance it always had - table settings perfect with crisp linen and sparkling cutlery. Front of house skills are obvious and the quality of food was consistent throughout the meal - the diner's high expectations are fully met with depth of flavour and sauces. Willie's motto of "taste is the key" with flavour and presentation has always been his trademark and he brings the best out of good basic ingredients. As indicated by me last year other agencies would soon recognise this establishment and already (only re-opened in May 2002) the AA have awarded the accolade of **Restaurant of the Year (2003-04) Scotland and Northern Ireland**. True testament to a first class operation.

Open: *Closed Sun/Mon, Sat lunch.*	**Smoking:** *Bar area only.* **Covers:** *50*
Xmas & New Years Day.	**Price Guide:** *Lunch from £12.00-£25.00*
No Rooms: *N/A*	*Dinner £34.00-£38.00*
Children: *Yes*	**Location:** *Turn left at mini r/about at end of Elderslie Street*
Disabled: *Dining on ground level.*	*On left in Argyle Street.*

LA BONNE AUBERGE

161 West Nile Street, Glasgow G1 2RL.
Tel: 0141 352 8310   Fax: 0141 352 7447.
email: contactus@labonneauberge.co.uk

This was the original Brasserie opened in 1975 by hotelier and restaurateur Maurice Taylor and today it still forms an integral part of the city's exceptional restaurant scene. The ethos behind this project was the brasserie concept in its purest form. This is quality French Mediterranean cuisine served in comfortable and relaxed surroundings. This restaurant, although part of the Holiday Inn Theatreland, stands on its own merit and pre-theatre dining is a must - head chef Gerry Sharkey demonstrates good technical skills - simple but uncomplicated dishes with a certain amount of innovation and a french influence. Casual dining or an excellent table d'hôte menu (2 or 3 course) available with good choice of wines. Private dining can be arranged (exclusive use) in the Mon Marte suite - ideally placed for the The Royal Concert Hall nearby. 1 AA red rosette for food. Food & Beverage Manager Aiden Livingstone. *AA*✿

Open: *All year*	**Smoking:** *Designated area.*
No Rooms: *N/A*	**Covers:** 110
TV in Rooms: *N/A* **Room Tel.** *N/A*	**Price Guide:** *Lunch: £6.95 - £10.95*
Children: *Yes*	*Dinner: £12.95 - £25.00 (pre theatre)*
Disabled: *Yes*	**Location:** *Opposite Royal Concert Hall.*

STRAVAIGIN

28 Gibson Street, Hillhead, Glasgow. G12 8NX
Tel: 0141 334 2665   Fax: 0141 334 4099.
email: bookings@stravaigin.com   www.stravaigin.com

This restaurant and cafe bar is the domain of Colin Clydesdale - a name synonymous with food in Glasgow. Situated in the busy west end of Glasgow the restaurant occupies the basement beneath the cafe bar - this provides the option of a more comprehensive menu or a quick meal in the cafe bar. The bistro type atmosphere is prevalent throughout - informality with genuine Glasgow hospitality. Your choice could include seared scallops, roast oriental duck with a soba noodle strudel and mango coriander jus - to finish a chocolate cherry bread pudding with white pepper ice-cream and cherry compote. Ever changing menus and options are available - Colin uses his culinary skills to introduce new dishes with great success - this is reflected in the 2 AA red rosettes awarded to this establishment and Stravaigin was voted best restaurant of the year in 1998 by The Scottish Chefs Association. *AA*✿✿

Open: *All year ex. 25/26/31st Dec. Jan 1st. Sun Lunch*	**Smoking:** *Upstairs only.*
No Rooms: *N/A*	**Covers:** 76
TV in Rooms: *N/A* **Room Tel.** *N/A*	**Price Guide:** *Dinner: 2 courses £22.95 3 courses £27.95*
Children: *Yes*	*Lunch: from £12.95*
Disabled: *Unsuitable*	**Location:** *M8, junct 17 or A82 from city centre - Gt Western road, turn down park road,'rt into Gibson St., 200 yds on right*

THE CROSS AT KINGUSSIE

Tweed Mill Brae, Ardbroilach Road, Kingussie PH21 1TC
Tel: 01540 661166   Fax: 01540 661080
email: relax@thecross.co.uk   www.thecross.co.uk

This restaurant with rooms is synonymous with quality. It nestles comfortably in 4 acres of attractive woodland and garden beside the river Gynack - formerly a water powered tweed mill it has been restored and extended to provide 8 stylish bedrooms and a contempory restaurant. Original features have been retained and the building has great character. The ambition (and dream) of new Scottish owners David & Katie Young was finally realised and they have managed the transition extremely well. (Hampshire to the Highlands!!) David's experience as an AA senior food inspector will come in handy here. An important step was retaining the services of Becca Henderson from the previous régime - she and David are a formidable duo in the kitchen. Have been here on 4 occasions already (on my doorstep) - obviously great dedication here, mastery of techniques and a clear ambition to achieve high standards - dining expectation fully realised. Choice of 2, 3, or 4 course - prices include appetiser, coffee & service. Relaxed and friendly ambience - AA top 200 places to stay in the UK, AA 2 red rosette award for food and RAC Blue Ribbon. *AA* 🏵 🏵

Open: *All year ex. Xmas, New Year, Jan*	**Smoking:** *Designated area*	**Covers:** *24*
No Rooms: *8 (all en suite)*	**Price Guide:** *Rooms £130.00-£240.00 (incl dinner)*	
TV in Rooms: *On request* **Room Tel.** *Yes*	*Dinner £28.50-£38.50*	
Children: *Yes*	**Location:** *Centre of village at traffic lights - uphill along*	
Disabled: *Dining only*	*Ardbroiloch Road. 250 yds turn left down drive.*	

LIVINGSTON'S RESTAURANT

52 High Street, Linlithgow, West Lothian EH49 7AE
Tel: 01506 846565   Fax: 01506 846565
Email: alan@stevensons-scotland.com

This charming restaurant in Linlithgow has built up an enviable reputation and has consistently held the 2 AA rosette award - an indication in itself of the high quality of cuisine maintained by head chef Julian Wright. The charm is in the form of a "cottage" reached through a vennel off the main street which opens up into a wonderful garden setting and is the subject of a first prize awarded by the local authority. A family business there is emphasis of a personal note here coupled with excellent front of house service. Food prepared demonstrates excellent combinations and balance of ingredients with a consistency throughout all courses. Menus offer a mixture of signature and other innovative choices. Meals include Christine Livingston's legendary tablet and coffee. Plans are well advanced to extend the kitchen and add a new conservatory before Xmas. A very relaxed atmosphere here - previous winner of Scotland's "out of town" restaurant. Excellent wine list. Hosts: Ronald, Christine & Derek Livingston. *AA* 🏵 🏵

Open: *Closed Sun/Mon & 1st 2 weeks*	**Disabled:** *Yes*
Jan and 1 week June & Oct	**Smoking:** *No*
No Rooms: *N/A*	**Covers:** *50*
TV in Rooms: *N/A* **Room Tel.** *N/A*	**Price Guide:** *Lunch £13.50-£16.50 Dinner £27.00-£32.50*
Children: *Over 8 (evening)*	**Location:** *Eastern end of High Street opp. Post Office.*

THE WATERFRONT

No. 1 The Pier, Oban, Argyll PA34 4LW.
Tel/Fax: 01631 563110
www.waterfront-restaurant.co.uk

Don't be put off by the exterior of the building - the restaurant is on the first floor of the old seaman's mission on the "ferry to the Islands" pier. A bright and airy restaurant where everyone is there for the food. The emphasis is on fresh fish and seafood and a chalkboard lists the daily specials which are whatever comes in on the fishing boats that day. Carnivores and vegetarians are catered for as well. The brigade of chefs are on view in an "open" kitchen which helps create the ambience of the place. A typical meal might be seared scallops & langoustine tails (also main course if desired) pan fried sea bass and a homemade passion fruit cheesecake. Lighter meals of homemade crab & cod cakes available. The philosophy of the Waterfront is clearly stated as "from pier to the pan as fast as we can". A welcome addition to The Good Food Book. Proprietor: Annie Paul. Head Chef/Manager: Alex Needham.

Open: *All year (ex. Dec. 26th - Feb. 13th)*	**Smoking:** *No*
No Rooms: *N/A*	**Covers:** *76*
TV in Rooms: *N/A* **Room Tel.** *N/A*	**Price Guide:** *Lunch £8.00-£15.00*
Children: *Yes*	*Dinner £10.00 - £25.00*
Disabled: *No*	**Location:** *Head for ferry pier - signposted.*

CREEL RESTAURANT WITH ROOMS

Front Road, St. Margaret's Hope, Orkney KW17 2SL
Tel: 01856 831311
email: alan@thecreel.freeserve.co.uk   www.thecreel.co.uk

Although not quite on your doorstep this is a mecca for all who enjoy food prepared to consistently high standards on the south part of Orkney just over the Churchill Barriers and 14 miles from Kirkwall. The location adds to the rustic ambience of this seafront house overlooking St. Margaret's Hope. Chef proprietor Alan Craigie and his wife Joyce have been a permanent fixture here for many years building up such a reputation that The Creel has 2 AA Red Rosettes consistently held, over a number of years, for food. There is complete dedication here - food prepared using much of the island produce but with originality, flair and imagination that reflect a high quality of culinary skills. It could be described as modern cooking with a hint of Orcadian influence. A "restaurant with rooms" (new VisitScotland category) there are 3 en suite bedrooms - the ideal scenario to enjoy your food and stay awhile with a yarn and an excellent malt whisky. **AA** 🏵 🏵

Open: *Closed Jan/Feb. Open Apr-Sept & weekends Nov/Dec*	**Smoking:** *No throughout*
	Covers: *34*
No Rooms: *3 En Suite*	**Price Guide:** *B/B single from £40.00*
TV in Rooms: *Yes* **Room Tel.** *No*	*B/B double from £65.00*
	Dinner: from £27.00
Children: *Over 5* **Disabled:** *Unsuitable*	**Location:** *A961 South across Churchill barriers. 20 mins from Kirkwall*

BAIGLIE COUNTRY RESTAURANT

Aberargie, Nr. Bridge of Earn, Perthshire PH2 9NF
Tel/Fax: 01738 850332
email: Baiglieinn@aol.com

You will find this restaurant at the "bottom" of Glenfarg on the old road to Edinburgh from Perth a mile from Bridge of Earn - came upon this one by accident one day and after lunch my investigations led me to Master Chef/Proprietor Tom McConnell. After an apprenticeship at "The George Hotel" in Edinburgh Tom spent 20 years in Australia (Brisbane) and quickly built a name for himself rising to Captain of the Australian Culinary Team and National Master Chef. Since returning to Scotland, Tom gained membership to the National team for Scotland and worked at Gleneagles. Subsequently, with his wife Carol, he opened his own restaurant near Perth. I returned for dinner - there is no doubt of the talent here and a master of the kitchen - a high level of commitment, sound technical skills and a true exponent of fresh produce. Fine dining is supplemented (same quality) with bar lunches & suppers. Soon to be recognised by other agencies I am sure Tom describes his food as 5 star at 3 star prices. For the "foodies" don't miss this one out on your travels.

Open: *Closed first 3 weeks of April*	**Smoking:** *Bar and lounge only*	**Covers:** *35*
No Rooms: *N/A*	**Price Guide:** £17.00 - £21.00 *(2 or 3 course)*	
TV in Rooms: *N/A* **Room Tel.** *N/A*	*Option of bar lunches/suppers*	
Children: *Yes*	**Location:** *Exit 9 from A90. 1 mile along "Baiglie Straight"*	
Disabled: *Access only*	*towards Glenfarg.*	

LET'S EAT

77-79 Kinnoull Street, Perth PH1 5EZ
Tel: 01738 643377   Fax: 01738 621464
Email: enquiries @letseatperth.co.uk

My association with proprietors Tony Heath and Shona Drysdale go back to the 80s and last year another well known chef, Graeme Pallister, joined the team as head chef. Let's Eat is situated on the corner of Kinnoull/Atholl Street close to the North Inch and only minutes from Perth centre. There is a wonderful ambience within the premises and great expectation – this expectation is translated into cuisine at its very best – mainly Scottish with a continental influence. The blackboard specials are very popular but signature dishes include rack of lamb, roasted monk fish and breast of gressingham duck as main courses. Starters could include chowder of smoked haddock or warm salad of breast of pigeon. Finish with warm raspberry frangipan tart. Although many food accolades have been bestowed upon this restaurant over the years (and rightly so) the consistency over those years is testament to a true master of the kitchen. Awarded 2 red rosettes on a regular basis. *AA* ❀ ❀

Open: *All year except Sun/Mon &*	**Smoking:** *Lounge area only*	
2 weeks in both Jan. & July.	**Covers:** *60*	
No Rooms: *N/A* **En suite:** *N/A*	**Price Guide:** *Lunch £12.50*	
TV in Rooms: *N/A* **Room Tel.** *N/A*	*Dinner £22 (varies according to choice)*	
Children: *Yes* **Disabled:** *Yes*	**Location:** *Corner Kinnoull/Atholl Street near North Inch.*	

THE OLD ARMOURY

Armoury Road, Pitlochry, Perthshire PH16 5AP.
Tel: 01796 474281 Fax: 01796 473157
Email: angus@theoldarmouryrestaurant.fsnet.co.uk

Extremely attractive reclusive location nestling in woodland not far from the fishladder on the outskirts of the town with ample car parking. I have sampled chef/proprietor Angus McNab's food long before he arrived at Pitlochry. A previous winner of the Silver Quaich (Scotch Quality Beef & Lamb Association) Angus displays a dedicated approach with sound technical skills. These skills will soon be recognised by other agencies I am sure. Uncomplicated menus with excellent choice - clear and defined flavours with stocks and sauces. Under the supervision of Alison McNab the front of house team show their own skills - service is first class and a terrific ambience prevails throughout. Good wine list here to complement food of a very high standard. Delighted to include this restaurant in my Good Food Book. No smoking policy applies.

Open: *March - December*	**Smoking:** *No*	**Covers:** *48*
No Rooms: *N/A*	**Price Guide:** *Lunch £13.95 - £16.95*	
TV in Rooms: *N/A* **Room Tel.** *N/A*		*Dinner: a là carte £15.00 - £25.00*
Children: *Daytime only (Over 5 after 7pm)*		*(Lighter meals during the day)*
Disabled: *Yes*	**Location:** *Follow sign at north end of town.*	

THE PLOCKTON HOTEL

Harbour Street, Plockton, Wester Ross IV52 8TN
Tel: 01599 544274 Fax: 01599 544475
email: info@plocktonhotel.co.uk www.plocktonhotel.co.uk

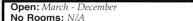

This village, popularised by the TV series about local policeman Hamish MacBeth is now known to most - unsurpassed location it has stunning views over Loch Carron to the Torridon mountains beyond. More a restaurant with rooms (classified hotel) and family run, the reputation of this establishment is well known for some of the best seafood (house speciality) in the land. The seafood platter a firm favourite but menus offer traditional dishes of venison, lamb, & beef. Other options include herring in oatmeal, Plockton smokies and vegetarian dish of the day. All dishes are of a very sound quality with emphasis on fresh food - mainly from their own doorstep. Recognised by all the main agencies this was awarded AA Best Seafood Pub in 2002 and AA Pub of the Year 2003. Well furnished and comfortable bedrooms with en suite facilities - two family suites available and a cottage annexe. Don't miss this one on your travels - a very relaxed and friendly atmosphere prevails throughout - your hosts Dorothy, Tom & Alan Pearson. Just north of Kyle of Lochalsh, the gateway to Skye. Highly recommended. Reports please.

Open: *All year ex. New Year's Day*	**Smoking:** *Designated area*	**Covers:** *60*	
No Rooms: *11 en suite*	**Price Guide:** *Lunch £12.00 - £15.00*		
TV in Rooms: *Yes* **Room Tel.** *Yes*		*Dinner £20.00 - £25.00*	
Children: *Yes*	**Location:** *Harbour Street - main road*		
Disabled: *Yes (Cat 2)*		*through village overlooking loch.*	

RESTAURANT MICHAEL DEANE

36-40 Howard Street, Belfast. BT1 6PF
Tel: 02890 560000 Restaurant: 02890 331134 Fax: 02890 560001
email: liz@deanesbelfast.com

I was fortunate to meet Michael Deane when he worked in the north of Scotland some years ago and sample his skills. At this stage his talents were not well known but it came as no surprise to hear of his reputation back in his native Belfast - he had opened his own establishment in 1997. His exhuberant style - both of showmanship and of uncompromisingly perfectionist cooking has elicited praise from the sternest of food critics and the most demanding food guides. Reluctant to classify his food - there are perceptible French, Pacific Rim, British and Irish influences in a typical menu - Michael Deane believes that it is the chef's imperative to set trends, rather than follow them. The secret is never to cease to innovate. From his beginnings at Claridges Michael has been on a pilgrimage - always propelled by his pure passion for food and its possibilities. AA 3 red rosettes. UK Good Food Guide. Keep this one in mind and follow this entry whenever in Belfast. *AA* ❀ ❀ ❀

Open: *Closed Sun.-Tues.*	**Disabled:** *Brasserie only*	**Covers:** *35*
No Rooms: *N/A*	**Smoking:** *No pipes or cigars*	
TV in Rooms: *N/A* **Room Tel.** *N/A*	**Price Guide:** *Dinner: £33.00 (2 courses)-£59.00*	
Children: *Welcome*	*Lunch: Brasserie - from £15.00*	

Brioche

Part One
Ingredients:
1 K strong flour
150g caster sugar
20g salt
25g yeast
12 eggs
400g unsalted butter

Method:
Mix all of the ingredients together except the butter. Mix this until it is well incorporated and the dough comes away from the bowl; slowly add the softened butter and allow to prove. Get two loaf tins, line with butter and greaseproof paper, place the dough equally into both tins. Allow to re-rise and place into a pre-heated oven at 200°C.

Blackberry Coulis
Ingredients:
2 punnets of blackberries
½ lemon juiced
50g caster sugar

Method:
Place a saucepan onto the stove, add all your ingredients and stir. Allow to break down on a low heat for 5-10 minutes. Bring off the stove and pass through a fine sieve.

Berry collection

1 punnet strawberries
1 punnet blackberries
1 punnet blueberries
1 punnet raspberries
2 sprigs mint

Set Vanilla Saboyon
Ingredients:
1 egg
40g caster sugar
1½ leaves of gelatine
250ml double cream
1 vanilla pod split in half
1 tsp vanilla extract

Brioche

Part Two

Method:

Place the sugar into a saucepan and place onto the stove; add enough water to cover it and bring to 150°C. Place the eggs into a mixing bowl and whisk until pale; Whisk in the sugar liquid until cold. Now, in a separate bowl, whisk the double cream vanilla pod, extract till it forms a soft peak and fold in the egg mixture. Place the gelatine into a saucepan with water just enough to cover and warm till disolved. Fold into the mixture and place into the fridge for two hours.

Dressing the Dish:

Cut the brioche into medium-sized discs; place the discs into a bowl with half the raspberry coulis. Now place one disc on to the plate and place some of the berries onto the disc; repeat twice more. Place three quenelles of vanilla Saboyon round the berries; drizzle blackberry coulis round the plate. Finally, place one piece of mint on top of the berries.

Chef: Daniel Richardson
Head Chef, The Loft Restaurant, Blair Atholl.
(also see entry page 79)

Medallions Of Venison With Wild Mushrooms

Ingredients:

12 x 60 g medallions of venison (fillet or saddle)
200 g fresh wild mushrooms
5 finely sliced shallots
2 small baking potatoes (unpeeled)
8 finely crushed juniper berries
bunch of flat leaf parsley, chopped
1 litre of strong game or beef stock
200 g plain flour, seasoned
2 tsp redcurrant jelly
125 ml port or red wine
sea salt
black pepper
100 ml olive oil
1 knob of butter

garnish: redcurrants, blueberries, raspberries
crispy celeriac (fine strips quickly deep-fried until golden brown)

Method:

In a saucepan, bring to the boil the litre of stock together with the port and the redcurrant jelly and reduce the volume by 2/3. Cut the potatoes into 2 cm thick slices, brush with a little olive oil and lay out on a baking tray. Sprinkle on some sea salt, black pepper and the crushed juniper berries and bake in the oven until golden brown and soft (220 °C for 15-20 min).

Sauté the shallots and mushrooms in 30 ml olive oil in a hot pan for approx 4 min. Add the chopped parsley and season with sea salt and pepper. Dip the venison medallions into the plain flour and cover until lightly coated. Shake off any excess and brown quickly in a hot pan with 30 ml of olive oil (about 30s each side). Bring the reduced stock back to the boil, add the butter and whisk until mixed through.

To arrange, layer three medallions of venison and two potato slices alternatively in the centre of the plate, starting with a medallion of venison at the bottom and finishing with the third on the top. Arrange the sautéed mushrooms around the plate and drizzle the gravy over the medallions. Garnish with berries and celeriac.

Chef: Hermann Schmid
Head Chef, The Crynoch at Lairhillock, Netherley, Stonehaven.
(also see entry page 77)

STEVENSONS

SCOTLAND'S
GOOD HOTEL AND FOOD BOOK
2004

Order Form: **Alan Stevenson Publications**
Fala, 14 Cairn Slowne, Osprey Grange, Aviemore,
Inverness-shire PH22 1LG
Tel: 01479 810714
Fax: 01479 811094
E-mail: alan@stevensons-scotland.com

Date: .... Please mail .... Copies of

Stevensons, Scotland's Good Hotel and Food Book, 2004.

Your Name: ....

Address: ....

.... Postcode: ....

Retail Price	1 Book	2-5 Books	6 + Books
United Kingdom	£7.50	£6.50 each	p.o.a.
USA only	$15.00	$12.00 each	p.o.a.
Canada only	$16.00	$13.00 each	p.o.a.
Europe	£7.50	£6.50 each	p.o.a.
Euro Zone	€12.00	€10.00 each	p.o.a.
Outside Europe	£10.00	£8.00 each	p.o.a.

Post & Packaging	1 Book	2-5 Books	6 + Books
United Kingdom	£1.50	£5.00	p.o.a.
USA/Canada	$9.00	$11.00	p.o.a.
Europe	£4.00	£7.50	p.o.a.
Euro Zone	€6.50	€10.00	p.o.a.
Outside Europe	£5.00	£4.00	p.o.a.

All orders outwith United Kingdom consigned by airmail. Payment in pounds sterling, please, payable to Alan Stevenson Publications - alternatively online at www.stevensons-scotland.com

No. of Copies: ...... at £/$/€ .... each. Total £/$/€ ....

Post & Packaging   Total £/$/€ ....

I enclose a Cheque/Bank Draft   Total £/$/€ ....

Hotels listed alphabetically by name

See contents page for list of Trade Sponsors.

I N D E X

Hotels continued

Restaurants listed alphabetically by name